# THE CHAKRA COOKBOOK

## COLOURFUL VEGAN RECIPES TO BALANCE YOUR BODY AND ENERGIZE YOUR SPIRIT

### ANNIKA PANOTZKI

NOURISH

EAT WELL, LIVE WELL

**The Chakra Cookbook**
Annika Panotzki

Originally published as *Regnbågsmat* in 2018
by Norstedts, Stockholm.
Published in agreement with Barrling Intl.
Literary Agency.

First published in the UK and USA in 2022 by
Nourish, an imprint of Watkins Media Limited
Unit 11, Shepperton House,
83–93 Shepperton Road
London N1 3DF

enquiries@nourishbooks.com

Commissioning Editor: Ella Chappell
Assistant Editor: Brittany Willis
Head of Design: Karen Smith

Senior Designer: Kate Cromwell
Production: Uzma Taj
Commissioned artwork: Vira Kiktso
Commissioned photography: Magnus Ragnvid
Author photography on page 7: Sofie Wilberg

A CIP record for this book is available from the
British Library

ISBN: 978-1-84899-405-8 (Hardback)
ISBN: 978-1-84899-406-5 (eBook)

10 9 8 7 6 5 4 3 2 1

Printed in Bosnia and Herzegovina

Publisher's note:
While every care has been taken in compiling
the recipes for this book, Watkins Media Limited,
or any other persons who have been involved
in working on this publication, cannot accept
responsibility for any errors or omissions,
inadvertent or not, that may be found in the
recipes or text, nor for any problems that may arise
as a result of preparing one of these recipes. If you
are pregnant or breastfeeding or have any special
dietary requirements or medical conditions, it
is advisable to consult a medical professional
before following any of the recipes contained in
this book.

Notes on the recipes – unless otherwise stated:
Use medium fruit and vegetables
Use fresh herbs, spices and chillies
Use coconut sugar where possible
Do not mix metric, imperial and US cup
measurements:
  1 tsp = 5ml  1 tbsp = 15ml  1 cup = 240ml

nourishbooks.com

# CONTENTS

# INTRODUCTION

We live in a culture where we turn our backs on ourselves when it comes to our own health. It is time to trust the ability we already have within us. I meet so many people every day who express that they are tired of performing, of stressing themselves out trying to live up to a standard of perfection that we have been led to believe will bring happiness. We have tried this way of living for many years and are beginning to understand that everything is actually about the inside. If we do not feel good in body and soul, there is no designer bag or luxury holiday in the world that can fill that hole. First, we need to build up our energy, give ourselves love, peace and a pat on the back. Then we can buy the bag if we want, just because it looks good, and not to fill the emptiness. Raising one's energy is about being more true to oneself, listening to the body and to the gut feeling.

I want to show you that when you follow your inner voice you invite more ease, joy, energy and health into your life. This book's intention is to be an inspiration to find your own way to do it. I want to remove all seriousness and invite creativity and joy, and to show that food and health are not so complicated when we rekindle our connection with nature.

In nature is a wisdom that we humans have lived by and enjoyed for thousands of years. We just need to remember that wisdom again. We are part of this planet, and in nature there is everything we need to heal, stay healthy and reach our highest potential. It is natural that we want to be filled with energy and constantly renew ourselves.

I just want to remind you of what you already know in your heart …

# ANCIENT WAYS OF THE SHAMAN IN A MODERN WORLD

It is easy to lose the connection to the natural world when we live in a city and have a busy life. But it is important to remember that our physical bodies represent the natural world and the elements. The root chakra is representing the feminine earth and the sacral chakra her waters. In the solar plexus comes the sun and the fires, and the heart chakra contains the wind, to be able to fly like an eagle. To create life here on earth they are all needed. It is all woven between the sacred feminine and the sacred masculine; the love story of the earth and the sun that creates lives. We are a microcosmos of the same principles. What we do to our bodies we do to the earth; if we respect and love the earth, we respect and love ourselves. It is all connected. Every little being and plant here on this planet is created by the same force. It is easier to see when we live close to nature and when we live by her cycles.

To reconnect to our bodies and spirits we need to reconnect to nature. Heal the relationship with our greater mother. She is the one that gave us life so we need to honour her and all of her creations. Every tree, every plant, all the animals and each other. When we heal this connection, we activate our root chakra and foundation again. On this foundation we can build a new connection and inner self. This foundation starts with self-love, just as it reflects our love for Mother

Nature. A mother's love is unconditional. That kind of love can see perfection in everything and have humble, warm eyes for her child. That creates a safe environment to thrive on. A love to be grateful for and honour. This is how we need to look at ourselves and our bodies: through that unconditional loving sight. We honour ourselves by giving ourselves food, thoughts, actions and rest that our bodies can use to heal, refuel and reenergize. Natural food from our Mother Nature, already created so perfectly to match our cells since we are connected to the earth and all is one.

We have forgotten to say thank you for all the gifts that she brings us, all the love that she gives, no matter how we treat her. She is here unconditionally. This is the way of ritual. We can bring ritual into our modern life in small ways during the day. When we honour ourselves we honour Mother Earth. A few minutes in the morning to do some breathing exercises, to thank ourselves, to put forth loving intentions, to give ourselves natural beautiful food, to give thanks for that food, to put a flower on her belly (the earth), to laugh and to live with an open heart. To support each other and all living beings by creating more peace, balance and love.

Even in the city you can live by the cycles of the moon, as we did in ancient times. When the moon is full it is time to give thanks for what has created itself and give closure to what no longer is needed. In a modern way, see how you can declutter your home from unnecessary things, projects and relationships that bring you down. Close doors to old habits. Honour yourself with a beautiful flower bath and nourishing infusions. Give thanks and closure to what no longer brings joy to your life and soul.

The week after the full moon you just keep on nourishing and honouring yourself. When the energy of the new moon comes it is time for a renewal – a cleanse like the 5-Day Reset in this book, taking on new projects, creating and activating. A ritual to bring in the new. Asking the universe to support your destiny path. To bring in more joy and passion. The following week is to take small actions to really support your visions of the new.

Live by the cycles and honour yourself with rest and more quiet time after a more lively and exuberant time. Listen to your body in how to support these cycles. Eat seasonal produce. Support your body with different superfoods depending on your personal needs. It doesn't have to be a big thing to matter. It will feel so good to live with that balance. Even if we don't live on a mountain or in the rainforest we can still take the essence and incorporate it into our lives.

What kind of a world do we want to leave for our future generations? It all starts with us. The responsibility for our own health, our choices, our actions. To listen to that inner guidance of our own intelligence. Our body and soul already know how to create balance. They tell us every moment through our gut feeling. Just relearn how to listen. You are a master healer and all it takes is trust and self-love. One step each day takes you far. We are here to enjoy life fully and to live in health and balance. When we support ourselves, life starts to support us and we co-create with nature and each other.

It is the way of the heart, where all is connected and we find a higher meaning to this life and this planet. Together we thrive! We become the rainbow beings. Together, all of the colours are white, like the inside of a clear crystal and a prism. We become the light.

# EAT THE COLOURS OF THE RAINBOW

We are equipped with our five senses for a reason. They help us navigate through life, experiencing this world. When we eat and drink, we want to satisfy all our senses and our entire energy system. Many ancient cultures, for example in Asia and India, build each meal with flavours and colours in mind.

On the plate we want to stimulate our senses with all the colours of the rainbow, different scents, textures. Then we can be sure that we eat a varied diet and get the nutrition we need. A simple rule is to stay as close to the source (nature) as possible.

Nature creates our bodies, and our cells have an almost identical structure to those of a plant. Therefore, this energy and nutrition is easily absorbed. Our cells do not recognize a material that is produced chemically, and these are therefore not received by the body. This then instead becomes a "waste product", which the body must put its energy into getting rid of. The body is equipped to constantly cleanse itself of "heavy energy", meaning all residues, waste and chemicals that do not benefit it. It is a process that takes place right down to the cellular level, and thanks to it, the body stays healthy. When we overload the body with too much heavy energy and chemicals, this wears on our cleansing organs and it pollutes our blood. You can compare the blood in our body with all the water that flows here on earth. It is the water that gives all life – without water, no life. If we pollute our water, it becomes a breeding ground that causes the streams to silt up, the environment to become acidified and bad bacteria to grow stronger and eventually take over. An imbalance arises and our soil and crops become sick and deficient in nutrients. Exactly the same thing happens inside our body. Fresh blood, plenty of nutrition and good circulation provide healing and easily transport the nutrition to all organs that may do the job for which they are intended. Quite easy, actually. There is an illusion that it is boring to eat healthily, or that it is expensive with organic vegetables and fruits. These thoughts are really just something we have created in our minds. It is learned "truths" that are repeated. For a plate that explodes with colour, flavour, healing spices and exciting

> ON THE PLATE, WE WANT TO STIMULATE OUR SENSES WITH ALL THE COLOURS OF THE RAINBOW, AND WITH DIFFERENT SCENTS AND TEXTURES.

herbs, is it boring? If we rewind the tape, it is all basically about the relationship with yourself: the love for yourself and your own self-worth. The stronger this bond to yourself is, the more obvious it becomes to give yourself the best energy, energy that you know supports your body and that keeps you on top. It is also about a balance.

When we stop looking at the world in black and white, stop putting labels on everything, and put an end to all these bans in food and drink, we can instead focus on a simple formula. Good energy gives the right balance. When we remove everything complicated around this, it becomes easy to live by. We are often so obsessed with performance and demands that we place on ourselves that we sabotage our own lives. Think about how much energy is wasted by constantly keeping track of what everyone else is doing and what everyone else is going to think and feel. Save that energy for joy and creativity in your own life instead and learn to navigate with your energy. If you feel good about a glass of quality red wine from time to time, and if it gives you an uplifting joy, then no one else needs to think anything about it.

Of course, it is important to know your own balance and energy and where to draw the line when the uplifting becomes heavy, negative and stressful for the body. Ask yourself how you live your life on other planes. Is there a balance between food, movement, fluid, stillness, nature, etc.? When you have increased your energy so that the body is wonderfully balanced, various factors such as stress or heavier food do not affect it to the same extent. Only you can feel and regulate that balance. Be honest with yourself in all situations and follow the body's signals. If you have crossed your line, balance with the opposite energy. For example, if you have eaten very heavy, high-energy food during the day which has made you tired, bloated and low, you can eat light, liquid and uplifting food the next day. In this way, you support the body and regain balance before it has gone too far. Eventually, it becomes natural for you to balance these energies daily and respond more quickly with exactly what you need.

# YOUR ENERGY SYSTEM AND THE CHAKRA SYSTEM

Our physical body consists of atoms which in turn consist of energy. On this we can all agree. To keep this energy together, there are seven major energy centres which control certain areas and organs inside our body. The ancient wisdom traditions call this the chakra system. This system also stores information. As the body's cells are constantly renewing themselves, there is a fantastic potential to change and influence this information. We can do this through our thoughts, feelings, behaviours, and through what we eat and drink. In the same way that we are made up of energy, foods such as fruits, vegetables, nuts and grains are also energy.

Each energy has a different vibration. Of course, chemically produced food also has an energy but with a different vibration. Getting to know your own energy system and knowing what is vibrating right for your body is the key to good health. Our bodies are created from an enormous natural intelligence and equipped with everything we need to navigate to a perfect balance. The ancestors who lived close to nature and followed its cycles had a highly developed navigation system, which we can call intuition. Some would call it gut feeling. The body is so intelligent that immediately after a meal it lets us know how this food was received. It's really quite simple. When the body signals that it has become energetic, light, satisfied, uplifted, or if you get a good feeling, then it is the right energy for you in the food and drink. When the body reacts by making you feel heavy, dizzy, tired, drowsy, bloated and uncomfortable, the energy is not right.

The cleaner your body is (i.e. the fewer chemicals, white sugar, hardened fat, artificial flavours and processed foods you take into your body), the stronger the signals you get, which are easier to interpret. As you become more balanced, your body is naturally drawn to good energy. You will know that it is a reliable source of energy, which builds, heals and strengthens the organs and other bodily functions. Then you can think further about the season, soil quality and which companies handle the raw material. Positive energy attracts more positive energy. In this way, your whole life can change so that you feel more joy, zest for life, creativity and health. When you feel good about yourself, you also naturally choose people and situations in your life that make you feel good. It will be a snowball effect that is rolling in a new, positive direction.

Every human being is unique, just as our fingerprints show. There is no one-size-fits-all template. But you can learn to listen to your own navigation system and your unique energy. Then you can once and for all be satisfied with your body, stop beating yourself up and instead create a loving relationship with yourself – an energetic and healthy relationship that lasts a lifetime! In the next chapter, you will gain a deeper insight into each chakra and inspiration for how to strengthen each energy. As I mentioned earlier, we do not create health with just one component, but you can strengthen overall health by looking at the totality of your energy system. Eating varied, colourful foods that nourish all chakras is one component, another is to see if each chakra gets to express itself. For example, if you constantly go about with a sore throat and cough, you can tune in to what may be out of balance in the throat chakra. Maybe you do not say out loud what you think and feel, but swallow injustices. Then you can consciously practise saying out loud what you feel and think. During this phase, you can consume more foods that strengthen this specific centre. If you feel in balance, you need only to maintain that balance.

**Crown Chakra**

**Third Eye Chakra**

**Throat Chakra**

**Heart Chakra**

**Solar Plexus Chakra**

**Sacral Chakra**

**Root Chakra**

# THE CHAKRAS FROM A SHAMANIC PERSPECTIVE

Our energy body, or the light body, is attached to our physical body through energy points, what we call chakras. Each chakra represents different energy, force, emotions, physical organs and their functions. The light body carries information about how to build our body, our mind and our emotional body. If something becomes imbalanced, either in this life, other timelines (past lives), or in our ancestral lines, it will be there as an imprint. This imprint can either be active or sleeping and is what attracts energy from our subconscious. You can see it manifested in patterns, for example, in relationships, friendships, work or health. These are the programmes that, in the example of relationships, can keep you attracting the same kind of partner. These imprints guide you when you ask yourself questions like "Why is this happening?" when you can't see what something has to do with a subconscious wound or programme. Different wounds and programmes are linked to different chakras, because the chakras also represent our stages in life.

The root chakra is the energy from when we came into this earth and our early years; how our needs were fulfilled and the unconditional love that we got. If something did go out of balance here, our root chakra will be affected. This is our connection to feeling held, safe, loved and cared for. Symbolically this is also our connection to Mother Earth and the sacred feminine. It's how we express our wild life force and creativity. The root chakra is the foundation, our soil that we build the rest of our energy system on. Your childhood is also an age where you are very sensitive to your environment. What you experience, and the programmes of your mother and father, becomes your truth.

The sacral chakra symbolizes the strong tree trunk that grows from the roots in the fertile soil. When we come into our teenage years, we start to get to know our power and strength. We challenge our inner powers by exploring the polarity between the feminine and masculine powers. If we have chosen strict parents, we often get help by our inner "archetype of the rebel" to break free. Here we need to find the balance within ourselves and in our life. This is the dance between the polarities. Symbolically we find our inner love story. If we lose our power in this important phase or become imbalanced, we can either go into victimhood, abuse our powers, or lose our power by being the saviour. We start to project our inner wounds and imbalances onto the outer world, and here we have the fight of the ego. We identify the ego or get caught in it; we can free ourselves of the projections or be misled by them. We have a chance to start trusting ourselves and our gut feeling, no matter what.

Our solar plexus is the seat of our soul. The voice of our essence. To reach the path of

our destiny, we first must free ourselves and transform the root and sacral chakras into pure power that supports our destiny. With the compass of the sacral chakra and the trust of our inner guidance, we can now thrive. We can allow our passion and creativity to fire up our dreams and not let anything stop us. We become vibrant and shining like the sun. Sourcing from a place of no ego, we listen to our inner wisdom and bring more joy and meaning to life. When all of us follow our inner passion and destiny, together we automatically create a new world. This is the seed we come to earth with and our path is to discover our inner gift to give and share with the world.

When we live from a higher meaning, we activate our heart chakra. We go beyond all of the judgements and no longer create just for ourselves. When our own cup is filled with unconditional love, oneness and forgiveness, it overflows to the world. We see that all is a part of the creation and a higher plan. The lessons that were needed are learned and we see the gold that is hidden in them: lessons, wisdom, expansion of the heart. We create a higher vision for future generations.

The throat chakra is where we radiate our inner truth and expression. When the inner work is balanced we no longer have the need to be right, lie, create conflict or gossip. This chakra helps us to become transparent. We are who we say that we are, and we do what we say we will do. There is nothing to hide and nothing to fight, just our inner truth in a calm, powerful expression. When you have that embodied, you don't even have to vocalize the boundaries that keep your energy intact – you radiate them. The energy of the Grandmother Moon helps to keep this chakra clear and brings magic into life. For it to happen she teaches us how to transform every month, to let go of what's no longer serving our inner truth and make room for something new. Her wisdom knows when it is time to sow and when it is time to reap.

Our higher selves and inner wisdom are connected to the third eye chakra. When we understand that we are our own healers, that we have all the answers within us, and what powerful manifestors we are, here is our connection between the worlds. With our inner eyes we can visit the different realms and dimensions, travelling to the Under World, Middle World and Upper World to find answers, gifts and download visions. With an open third eye chakra we can do the seemingly impossible and develop skills and senses beyond our five earthly ones. This is how we develop a communication with our higher selves, with the cosmos and our star families. We understand how everything is connected between the worlds.

The crown chakra is connected with the source of all, the universal source. It is like an antenna towards the cosmos. Every step that we take we create from within, like a movie that is written in every moment. If we source from a lower consciousness, we believe that outer circumstances are creating it for us and we let the subconscious, the programmes and the imprints dictate our movie. When we free ourselves and understand that we are the creators, we create every moment into reality.

When we build our energy system and find tools to keep the chakras in balance, we build a rainbow bridge from our bodies. That bridge keeps us connected with our inner selves and our higher self. One foot in each world.

# THE ROOT CHAKRA

**ELEMENT**
Earth

**COLOUR**
Red

**ENERGY**
The root chakra is our connection with nature and feminine energy. It is characterized by our early years here on earth and all that it has meant both socially and in terms of needs. This is where we lay the foundation for our security, self-esteem, sense of context, and belonging. The feminine energy is caring, fertile, nourishing and receptive. It is a wild, creative force with which we can create our lives. Here are also our basic instincts. Food, housing, reproduction and survival are in focus.

**OUT OF BALANCE**
When the root chakra is unbalanced, it can feel as if we cannot find our place here on earth, that we do not belong. We might feel fears of survival and lack of resources. We collect things to feel false security or seek confirmation outside ourselves through material things. We are afraid of being deceived or losing what we have. We believe we need to protect ourselves from the external world that appears to be "dangerous". We are out of sync with sexual needs and can easily become aggressive. We may also feel chronic fatigue.

**BODY**
The body's ability to eliminate residues and waste. Hormone production of oestrogen and testosterone. Various diseases and imbalances concerning areas such as the rectum, bones and feet.

**HOW TO BALANCE**
Spend more time in nature and serenity. Take care of yourself a little more, with, for example, a massage or a yoga class. Keep regular routines with food and sleep.

**FOODS**
beetroot/beet
blood orange
cherry
cranberry
goji berry
lingonberry
pomegranate
radish
raspberry
red apple
red chilli
redcurrant
red pepper
red rice
rhubarb
schisandra
strawberry
tomato
watermelon

*Other non-red root-chakra foods*
chaga mushroom
eucalyptus
garlic
maca
onion
peppermint
potato
reishi mushroom
rice
seeds
spruce shoot
sprouts

# THE SACRAL CHAKRA

**ELEMENT**
Water

**COLOUR**
Orange

**ENERGY**
The sacral chakra is our seat for the emotions and our inner power, and how we choose to use our power and manifest it. How we are with our flow in life. Here we can create balance, process all our emotions and choose how we walk here on earth. We want to go beyond all fears and illusions. In the sacral chakra, we strengthen our intuition and gut feeling.

**OUT OF BALANCE**
Fear and anger. Hard to forgive and move on. Need for control that is often expressed through money, manners, lust for power and sex.

**BODY**
Adrenal glands. Cortisol secretion, norepinephrine and adrenaline. Our fight-or-flight response.

**HOW TO BALANCE**
Be more in the water element. Drink more water, take long baths, walk along streams and listen to water sounds. Water purifies and balances emotions. Practise not going against the gut feeling. Practise not saying yes when you want to say no. Stand firmly for your opinions and thoughts without creating conflicts or drama.

**FOODS**
- apricot
- carrot
- cloudberry
- nectarine
- orange
- orange paprika
- papaya
- peach
- persimmon
- rosehip
- sea buckthorn
- turmeric

*Other non-orange sacral-chakra foods*
- vanilla

# THE SOLAR PLEXUS CHAKRA

**ELEMENT**
Fire

**COLOUR**
Yellow

**ENERGY**
The solar plexus is our energy bank in the body, the fuel to complete and realize our inner dreams. Joy, passion and saying YES to life. Here we go beyond all fears and dare to spread our wings in full confidence. We only engage in things that give us strength and nourishment. We do not waste our energy on what does not bring spiritual joy. We have the courage to respond to our calling in this life, a calling that is not just for personal gain, but benefits all living things on earth.

**OUT OF BALANCE**
Difficulty processing grief. Getting caught up in a victim's role or having too much pride to forgive and move on. This is also our seat of shame and guilt, and we can abuse our power by becoming manipulative or destructive.

**BODY**
Pancreas. Produces insulin that helps to extract glucose from the blood into the cells. Balances our glycaemic index. Also affects our liver. With problems in this energy centre, we often suffer from chronic fatigue because the body cannot fully extract nutrients from the food we eat before it is eliminated from the body.

**HOW TO BALANCE**
Refill with sunlight as much as possible. Sitting by a fire also gives this chakra new power. Make a list of things that bring joy. Small, simple, everyday things are good. Engage one of these every day. Listen to what the soul wants to say. What is the bigger dream that wants to be incorporated? See what is possible. Do something every day that brings you closer to your dream.

**FOODS**
- banana
- baobab
- ginger
- lemon
- maize
- mango
- passion fruit
- pineapple
- star fruit
- yellow beetroot/beet
- yellow courgette/zucchini
- yellow melon
- yellow pepper

*Other non-yellow solar-plexus-chakra foods*
- camu camu
- cinnamon
- clove
- cordyceps

# THE HEART CHAKRA

**ELEMENT**
Air

**COLOUR**
Green

**ENERGY**
This chakra is the path of the heart and love. Being able to give and receive love, beyond judgements, drama and negativity. We open ourselves up to trust and intimacy. Here we look at the world with warmth, love and humility. And here we also know that we are all created from the same source and are the same energy in different expressions – we are all brothers and sisters. We are hopeful, selfless and no longer seek happiness outside of ourselves but feel freedom and peace. What we want is to return to a playfulness and innocence with life, and to wake up every day with a curiosity about what life offers us just on this day. We walk the path of love and love ourselves and our neighbour just the way we are created.

**OUT OF BALANCE**
Loneliness, rejection, disappointment and abandonment. Selfishness and self-centredness. We get caught up in self-criticism, and find it hard to be intimate in a relationship on all levels.

**BODY**
The circulatory system, heart, lungs and breasts.

**HOW TO BALANCE**
Every time we feel uncertain about decisions, we can sit in silence for a while, focusing on our Heart chakra. Ask your heart and an answer will come from the soul that is not based on what someone outside ourselves thinks. Strengthening the heart is also to perform a selfless act that gives us genuine joy, without having to get anything back.

**FOODS**
- avocado
- broccoli
- brussels sprout
- celery
- courgette/zucchini
- green apple
- green bean
- green leaves
- green tea
- kale
- kiwi
- lime
- matcha
- moringa
- pea
- pear
- spinach
- sugar snap pea
- wheatgrass

*Other non-green heart-chakra foods*
- chaga mushroom
- lavender
- raw cacao
- reishi mushroom

# THE THROAT CHAKRA

**ELEMENT**
The moon, the light

**COLOUR**
Light blue

**ENERGY**
The throat chakra relates to how we express ourselves here on earth, talk about ourselves and about others. Likewise, how we use our voice to manifest our dreams and make ourselves heard. The energy of the moon is about magic and opening the door to what we do not yet know – the unknown. It is about living in harmony with nature's cycles. It encourages us to let synchronicity into everyday life by having confidence in something higher.

**OUT OF BALANCE**
Difficulty making our voice heard. Expressing negatively about ourselves and others. Spreading gossip and lies. The feeling that life is out of sync and "going against us". Difficulty listening to others in a conversation, feeling it is more important to be right than to be understanding. Difficulty sleeping.

**BODY**
Mouth, oesophagus, throat and back of neck. The thyroid gland, the parathyroid gland. Temperature regulation in the body. The distribution of fuel in the body. Our body weight and how the body extracts vitamins from food.

**HOW TO BALANCE**
See which doors need to be closed in your life that no longer give you anything positive. It can be an old friendship that no longer feels uplifting, or a job that was rewarding from the beginning but now no longer feels developing and fun. Dare to be true to yourself and always express your truth. Talking positively about yourself and others strengthens your throat chakra.

**FOODS**
blackberry
blueberry
blue spirulina
spirulina

*Other non-blue throat-chakra foods*
ginger
kelp
lemon
lemongrass
lime
mint
nori
rosemary
sage

# THE THIRD EYE CHAKRA

**ELEMENT**
Ether

**COLOUR**
Indigo

**ENERGY**
The third eye is our own inner wisdom and higher consciousness. Here is the answer to all our questions. It represents tranquillity and serenity. We no longer seek wisdom outside of ourselves, but find it from our own existence and experience. We find a higher meaning with ourselves and life. We see that everything belongs together in a larger existence.

**OUT OF BALANCE**
Denial, depression, confusion, neuroses and stress-related symptoms.

**BODY**
The brain, eyes, nervous system.

**HOW TO BALANCE**
Meditate and engage inward focus to calm thoughts.

**FOODS**
- acai
- blueberry
- blue spirulina
- spirulina
- juniper

*Other non-indigo third-eye-chakra foods*
- chia
- coconut
- coconut water
- flaxseed
- lavender
- macadamia nut
- mandarin
- pecan
- pineapple
- raw cacao
- walnut

# THE CROWN CHAKRA

**ELEMENT**
Cosmos, pure energy

**COLOUR**
Violet

**ENERGY**
In the crown chakra, we are one with everything. Beyond our physical bodies. Beyond time and space. Back to the source of creation.

**OUT OF BALANCE**
Psychoses

**BODY**
Skin, brain, hormonal balance.

**HOW TO BALANCE**
Meditate to evoke the feeling of oneness with all life.

**FOODS**
- acai
- aubergine/eggplant
- blackberry
- blackcurrant
- blueberry
- blue corn
- chokeberry
- grape
- maqui berry
- plum
- red cabbage

*Other non-violet crown-chakra foods*
- coconut water
- lavender
- lemon
- lime
- mango
- pineapple
- rose

# A SUSTAINABLE RELATIONSHIP WITH EARTH

In times where we are awash with information about climate change, how the oceans are filling with plastic and how forests are being destroyed, it is clear we have lost our relationship with the earth. However, this relationship is needed to maintain our balance, and for us humans to feel good. It is easy to feel helpless when the problems seem so big and widespread, but we can instead choose to focus on small actions that can make a real difference.

In the beginning, we lived in small villages, in a close relationship with each other and the ever-changing nature. Then we got to know, respect and become one with nature's energy. We tuned in to the cycles, went to bed when dark fell and woke up at sunrise. We depended on nature's resources and gave back what was needed, so a balanced relationship emerged. Since everything was on a small scale, we did not have to upset this balance, but only took what we needed and felt grateful for what we received and worked for. A relationship of giving and taking.

> WE CAN TAKE THIS THOUGHT ONE STEP FURTHER AND ONLY USE NATURAL MATERIALS, NATURAL CLEANING METHODS, NATURAL HAIR- AND SKIN-CARE PRODUCTS, AND RECYCLE WHEN WE CAN.

Can we re-establish this balance even in a modern society when we do not always grow crops ourselves, but shop in grocery stores? How can we best leave the world to our children, grandchildren, and their children? Many indigenous peoples make important decisions based on how they leave the earth for future generations. We can take inspiration from their way of looking at nature. They go beyond the physical that we can see with the naked eye, and realize that everything is part of a whole. If we harm nature, in the long run we harm ourselves. Of course, you should not harm Mother Earth, which gives us all life and nourishment.

One way to relate and contribute on a personal level is to ingest natural food, created by nature, into our body. We can take this a step further and only use natural materials and natural cleaners. Nowadays, there is a wide range of products available, so we do not have to compromise on quality or results. It is not necessary to be "a special human being" to do these things. It

is not about placing oneself in a compartment, or giving oneself a label, but simply leaving a neat planet behind us for our children. It's easier than we think.

What we give our energy to grows stronger. Therefore, when we are going to invest our energy and our money, we need to be more aware. Supporting smaller entrepreneurs who run a business of passion and heart is also much more fun. The money you invest in a product is energy that you invest in the future. So ask yourself where you want to put your resources and in what direction you want to lead the world.

For example, palm oil has devastating consequences for the environment and contributes to the deforestation of rainforests. Despite this, a large percentage of all foods on the market have this oil in their products. We consumers have an incredible power to lift this. If we choose not to buy these products, a change will take place. But as long as we close our eyes to the problems and think that our choices do not affect the big picture, then absolutely nothing will happen. It is an easy way to make your voice heard and influence what the world will look like in the future.

We reflect what is happening on our earth. If we choose to pollute our own "inner water", our blood, with chemicals and artificial substances, this also leads to our water being polluted in nature. What is created by nature is also created for us and can therefore not be harmful.

Start by changing one thing at a time, just like with your diet. Make minor changes when you feel ready. We often have a notion that we cannot do without one or the other because we have a certain habit pattern. Dare to try something new! Do not make such a big deal of it. De-dramatize the whole thing and remember that your small contribution will be enormous if we all contribute together!

> **THE MONEY YOU INVEST IN A PRODUCT IS ENERGY THAT YOU INVEST IN THE FUTURE.**

# YOUR SELF-HEALING BODY

Our bodies are programmed to self-heal at a cellular level. Every day there is new potential to support this natural process in the body. Nothing is static in our bodies and their functions. It is often said that after one month we have replaced our skin and hair cells. After three months, we have replaced many cells in our internal organs and tissues, and after one year we have essentially replaced them throughout our entire body. This gives us endless opportunities to influence our health.

**DO NOT COMPROMISE ON WHAT DOES NOT FEEL RIGHT IN THE HEART. JUST LIKE WITH FOOD, ONLY YOU YOURSELF KNOW WHAT IS RIGHT FOR YOU AND WHAT MAKES YOU FEEL GOOD.**

Whatever life has been like until now, we can embrace the idea that what we do today affects our future. One thing is better than none. Health is not just a single component, such as food, but part of something bigger. It is our physical body, our mind and our soul. They all need to be in balance and work together. A person who has eaten healthily all their life but carries unprocessed grief or anger within themselves can still develop a disease. Grief and anger are also energy, which when left unprocessed can affect the body negatively. We have an inner compass that guides us to what is right for us. All we need to do is listen to and support the signals sent to us.

We support our body and soul through the following pillars:

- Eating a varied, plant-based and natural diet
- Having a good fluid balance
- Moving our bodies regularly
- Oxygenating the body (breathing exercises, being out in nature)
- Surrounding ourselves with people who lift us and give positive energy
- Saying YES to what we really want in the heart

Do not suppress heavy energy such as sadness, anger, pain or disappointment; instead give the feeling an expression (write it down on paper, blow it into a rock and throw it away, tell the person in question how you feel, or just acknowledge the feeling and let it exist without fixing it). These are human dilemmas that we all face from time to time.

We need to acknowledge *all* of our inner selves and that these things exist within us.

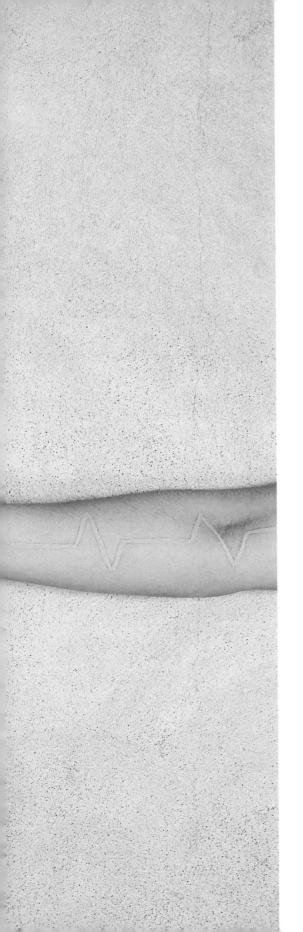

They are neither good nor bad. They are simply there. The more we learn to view ourselves in our entirety, without judgement, the less energy will be used to push away heavy emotions or project them onto others. This is a major energy problem that also settles as a stress in the body. When the body is under stress, not all of its organs function properly, and this also affects the hormone balance. Get to know yourself, your needs, and set boundaries.

Do not compromise on what does not feel right in the heart. Just like with food, only you know what is right for you and what makes you feel good. Find your own way to support your body and soul. Honour yourself and your time here on earth by not holding back who you really are. Honour your temple that gives you this amazing opportunity to experience our beautiful planet with all your senses. Ask yourself every day: How can I honour myself today? To be whole, healed, is to be oneself fully in all its expressions.

# CREATING BALANCE

We have all been in situations where we have gone against our body and our gut feeling. Perhaps the salty dinner with heavy ingredients felt tempting. Maybe we had already had a day filled with stress that made us tired. In that situation, the body is more easily attracted to fast carbohydrates to get fresh energy.

Be humble towards yourself. No one is perfect. We have all been there. If it has already happened, there is no reason to get caught up in what has already been. The focus is on the here and now. Light energy is needed to balance heavy energy.

This is what your recovery day might look like:

- Start the morning with an infusion for the sacral chakra (see page 160)
- Morning smoothie with cleansing superfoods
- A large green juice for lunch
- Energy-boosting smaller smoothie in the afternoon
- Soup for dinner
- A soothing nut milk

The following is a great way to let your body rest once a week or twice a month: Start the morning by sipping hot boiled water, decaffeinated tea or infusions once an hour until noon. It speeds up your digestion. The day after your fast, you can go back to lighter solid food again. If you feel you want to renew your energy, there is a suggestion for a five-day reboot later in the book.

During my years working as a health coach and energy healer, I have learned that those who adhere to the "black or white" mentality rarely maintain this lifestyle for a long period. It will be very short term because they have put in so much performance from the start. What is effective, however, is to get the ball rolling. It can be about exchanging your regular breakfast for a smoothie filled with superfoods. This new habit may give more energy in the morning, which gives a better mood and a lighter feeling in the body. When this new habit becomes an obvious part of your life, your newfound energy will naturally

> ## THIS NEW HABIT MAY GIVE MORE ENERGY IN THE MORNING, WHICH GIVES A BETTER MOOD AND A LIGHTER FEELING IN THE BODY

make you walk to work or choose a lighter meal for lunch that matches your new energy. In this way, you can slowly but surely bring in more health that is also sustainable.

Just like nature, we also have our cycles in expansion and contraction. Nature goes into expansion in the spring when everything germinates, and then fully during the summer when everything is in bloom. In the autumn, the contraction begins and then ends in the winter and the dormant phase. We can get to know our bodies in the same way and follow our own phases. Some periods are filled with extra energy, and we are creative, outgoing and want a lot around us. Other periods we are in phases where we prefer to be at home, take it easy and not have to exert ourselves.

In this way, you work with your body instead of against it. Resting phases are important for body and soul for renewal, then new energy gathers that can be directed towards achieving inner dreams.

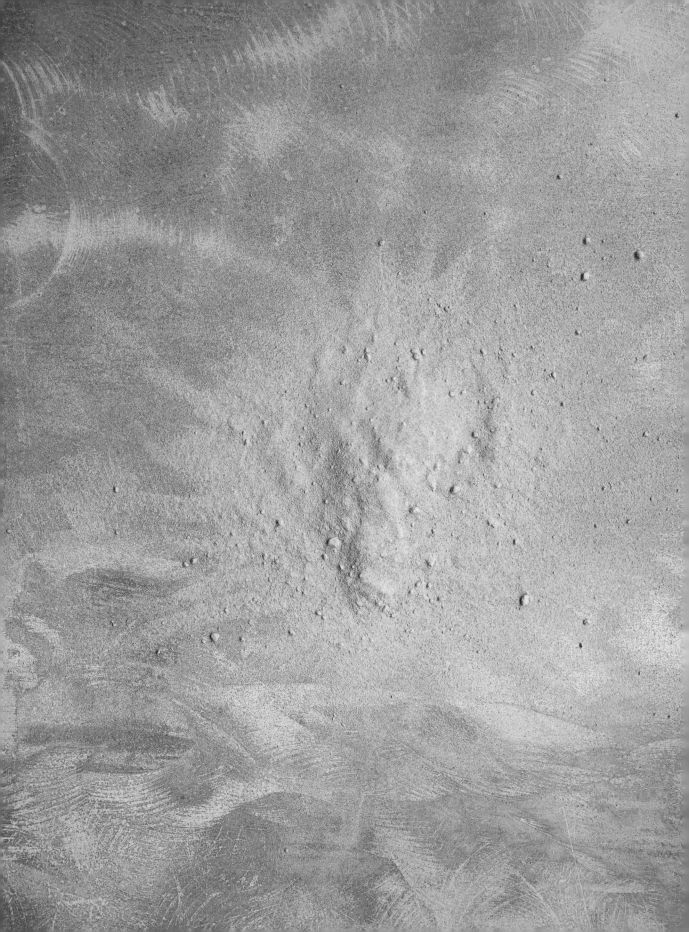

# JOY AND CREATIVITY

Life is too short to get caught up in demands and performance. Such things are not conducive to mental health.

Living healthily should not be for someone other than yourself. You experience life with your body and therefore you want to honour it by taking care of it. A healthy body gives you a calm mind and unlimited freedom. Once you have experienced this freedom, endless energy and joy, it is difficult to settle for less. Stop comparing yourself to others – live to your body's full potential. Walking around with pain, fatigue, low mood and a feeling of heaviness most of the time is not quality of life. You have the freedom to influence your own experience – is that not amazing? When something feels repetitive, static and boring, change it up. Eat other ingredients, sit on the floor to eat, choose a new way to work, travel to an unknown place outside your safety zone. Continue to be curious and exploratory. This gives genuine joy! There are endless ways to do things.

Once you have learned the principle of health, felt the power of being unlimited in your body and replenished with energy, it's time to get creative. Play with colours, spices, herbs and layouts. The same recipe can be varied endlessly when replacing a spice or ingredient. Do not be afraid to fail! Experiments create new flavours, and sometimes it is a hit. If you fail, you just have to move on to the next meal that has new potential. It's not that serious. Food should be fun!

The old teachings talk about creativity as a femi-force, viewing nature and Mother Earth as a creative feminine primordial force. The diversity in the plant kingdom, the animal kingdom and with us humans is infinite. You can find all the shades of the rainbow's colours, as well as unique structures, elements and qualities. In nature, nothing questions its potential to grow or live its purpose. And you can connect to this power and energy. Spend time in nature as often as you can and let this creativity inspire you!

> WHEN SOMETHING FEELS REPETITIVE, STATIC AND BORING, CHANGE IT UP. EAT OTHER INGREDIENTS, SIT ON THE FLOOR TO EAT, CHOOSE A NEW WAY TO WORK, TRAVEL TO AN UNKNOWN PLACE OUTSIDE YOUR COMFORT ZONE.

*PS ...* *As opposed to what you learned when you were little, play with food!*

## FOR FAMILIES WITH CHILDREN

A common question I have received over the years is how do I get my children to eat vegetables, superfoods and to live a healthier life. It's really quite simple: children do what we adults do and not what we say. If you show that food from nature is fun, creative and good, then it will be a truth for them. It does not have to be such a big deal; just let it be there completely naturally. Let the children be a part of exploring, feeling, tasting and cooking. They are completely fascinated by being able to turn vegetables and fruit into juices, or helping to create their own smoothie. As we give children green juices, they become used to the green flavours, and then eat many more greens in their natural form as well.

Over the years, I have discovered that contrary to our notions of "traditional" baby food, children love spices and a lot of flavour. I serve everything in small bowls so there will be many dipping sauces, finger foods and small dishes. Finger-friendly and fun to eat. Naturally, it can get a little messy. Do not give up if the children dislike something for the first time. Try another combination next time or try again after a while; it may take time to get used to an unfamiliar taste. Having a relaxed attitude to natural food and teaching children that they should always give themselves good energy sows a seed in them that will allow them to have a completely different relationship with their health and body in the future.

*PS ...*

*For those of you who do not have children: taste, play and enjoy the food and embrace its wonderful energy!*

## RITUALS IN YOUR EVERYDAY LIFE

A ritual is a way to focus your intention and then let the intention lead the energy. We, as humans, have this power. Whatever we focus our intention on grows stronger. That energy will attract more of the same energy. This is the law of attraction. We can consciously focus on more gratitude for what we already have and that will grow stronger. The more you give the more you shall receive. It's a way of co-creating with the universe. You can easily incorporate rituals and ceremonies into your daily life around your mornings, meals and evenings. You just amplify what you already do by adding small steps and an intention.

## WHEN YOU PREPARE YOUR FOOD

When you choose your food from the store, you can be aware of which fruit or vegetable is drawing your attention. If there are, for example, several different tomatoes, you can see which one you are intuitively drawn to. This is how your body's intelligence is resonating with that food. When you are about to prepare your meal, first tune into your heart and gratefulness. Then mindfully prepare the food from a place of love. This is going to get into your body so you want to infuse it with a loving energy. It is just a small mindset that is easy to apply, and the more you do it the more natural it feels. Arrange the food consciously on your plate to make it feel beautiful and vibrant. This is a gift to your body and an act of self-love.

## BLESSINGS

Before you eat or drink, take a moment just to attune to the energy on your plate or in your glass. Put one hand over the food or drink and the other hand on your heart chakra. Feel the gratitude for the food or drink. You can also thank the soil, the earth and the sun for its creation. Now ask the food to come into your body with nourishment and healing. Then tune into your heart and body, ask it to receive this food as nourishment and healing.

Really taste what you are eating and drinking. Enjoy it and feel how it is nourishing and healing your body, how your cells open up and receive. This will only take a few minutes and will change the whole way you look upon your body and food.

## TO CREATE A SMALL CEREMONY

A ceremony or ritual doesn't have to be complicated to have an effect. The most important thing is that you set an intention (see page 57) and that you do it with your heart. This is how a morning or evening ceremony could look:

You will need:
- a candle
- sage or palo santo incense
- flower petals, fresh or dried
- a herbal infusion for the chakra that you wish to strengthen (see page 160) or a chakra smoothie (see page 61)
- oracle card
- paper and pen

Method:
- Call in support from the universe to help you see what is needed.
- Create a cozy space and light a candle.
- Take the smoke from the sage or palo santo incense and cleanse your space to give it a good vibe.

- Make a flower mandala out of your flower petals. For each petal you blow in a wish/prayer or a blessing. Let your intuition guide you. There is no right or wrong. Just have a creative moment with your soul that awakens joy and a deeper meaning.
- Now take your infusion and connect with your heart. Feel the wish or blessing for yourself. Keep it in essence, like freedom, joy, creativity, peace. Blow it into your infusion or smoothie. Feel how it's already in your body and connect to that feeling. Now sip on your drink and feel how it infuses every cell in your body with this energy even further.
- Sit in stillness for a few minutes and in connection to this energy. Then draw an oracle card. Write a few sentences about what came up for you and set an action step for how to bring this essence into your life. For example, if the essence is freedom, it could be that you feel more free when in nature or by water. Then plan when you are going to make time for that. This is how we bring the essence into life. Energy attracts energy, so the more you are in that energy, the more you will attract it.
- Thank yourself and the space you have co-created with the universe's guidance.
- Close it by blowing out your candle.
- Take your message with you into the day or into your night's dreams.

# GOOD MORNING!

The early bird gets the worm. When we live close to nature and its natural rhythm, we wake up with it. It is the moment of the day when our thoughts are most still and we can get the power we need. Set your alarm a quarter of an hour earlier and create a calm morning ritual where you can set an intention for the day. Your morning can set the tone for your entire day. If you come out and meet the day feeling focused and calm, with a thought of how you want it to be, you can use your time in a new way. It is to honour oneself and one's time here on earth! Start your day with a large cup of morning infusion on an empty stomach and wait for 15–40 minutes before having your breakfast.

# MORNING INFUSION

Lemon is considered to have a very high vibration and helps the body's functions to get started. It activates the water energetically and makes the body better receive the hydration. The infusion acts as a rinse of the entire digestive tract and keeps your pH value in balance. Ginger has an anti-inflammatory effect and speeds up the metabolism. The period until your breakfast can be used for breathing exercises and to set an intention for the day. If you want to get an extra boost for your metabolism and increase your energy, you can also take a quick walk in nature before your breakfast.

YOU WILL NEED:
1 thick slice of organic lemon with peel
3cm/1¼in piece of fresh ginger, cut into pieces
300ml/10½fl oz/1¼ cups hot boiled water

> Put everything into a large cup or heatproof glass and let it steep for 5–7 minutes. Drink while it is still hot.

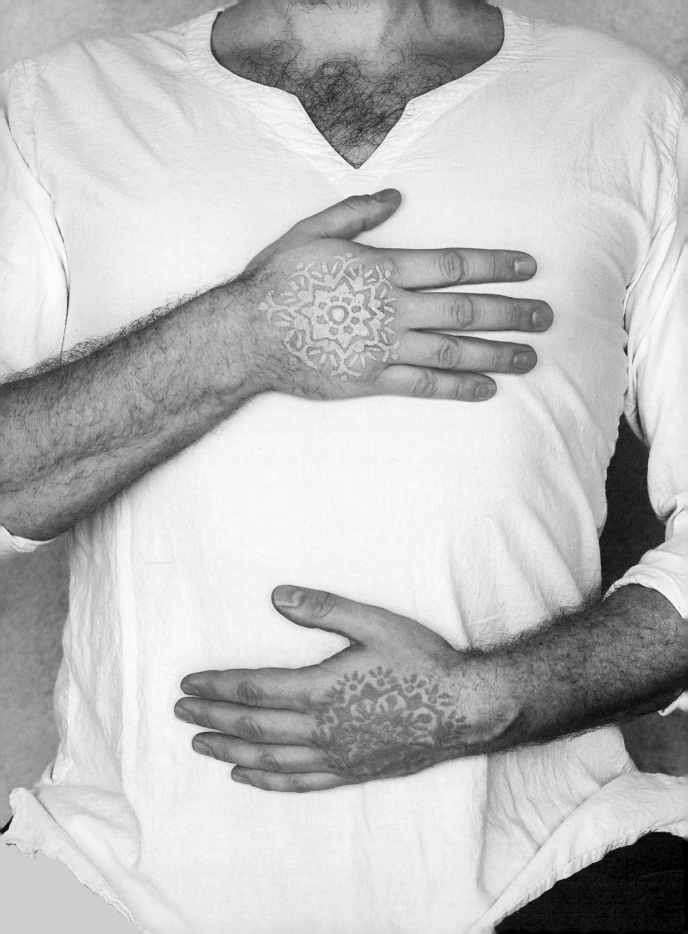

# PURIFYING MORNING BREATH

A major key to health is to keep the blood as oxygen-rich as possible because it provides good circulation and pH balance. With good circulation, the nutrients reach all organs, and all waste products in the body are carried out to the lymphatic system and then out of the body. This allows us to take in even more oxygen, and raise energy in the body. Out with the old, in with the new.

**STEP 1**

Sit in a comfortable sitting position where you can have a straight spine. Open the chest with the shoulders back and down. You can close your eyes to make it easier to get in touch with the breath.

**STEP 2**

Place the right hand on the heart chakra in the middle of the chest and the left on the sacral chakra, just below the navel.

**STEP 3**

Start by putting all your presence on the air that flows in and out through your nose, and just follow the breath. Continue to make the breaths deeper and longer. It should be as long an inhalation as an exhalation.

**STEP 4**

Follow the breath all the way down into the abdomen. Feel in your left palm how the stomach expands like a balloon when inhaled, and that the breath then continues all the way up and fills the palm towards the heart chakra. On exhalation, the air trickles from the top of the heart chakra and down to the stomach, where you squeeze out the remaining air while the navel goes towards the spine. Fill the stomach like a balloon again and repeat the procedure. Do at least 15–20 rounds.

For each inhalation, feel that new energy come in, and on exhalation, as if you're letting go of that which no longer benefits you.

**STEP 5**

Bring your awareness to the breath that flows in and out through the nostrils. Follow your breathing in and out through your nose until you are ready to slowly open your eyes again.

Abundance
Creativity
Freedom
Gratitude
Joy
Productivity
Love
Optimism

# MAKE AN INTENTION FOR THE DAY

After your morning breath and before you go out into your day, you can set an intention for the day. An intention is a direction of the energy that you want to attract into your life. Always keep an intention as an essence so as not to diminish the creativity of the universe. If you want more material success, do not focus on the material itself, but on the feeling of what it would mean for you. Examples of affirmations can be joy, freedom, abundance, and so on.

The important thing to note when setting an intention is that it comes from a feeling. Sit for a while and get in touch with your feeling. You can write your intention on a piece of paper to consciously bring down the energy into a physical form. In the evening, you can use your note and intention in a gratitude exercise that I describe later in the book (see page 166).

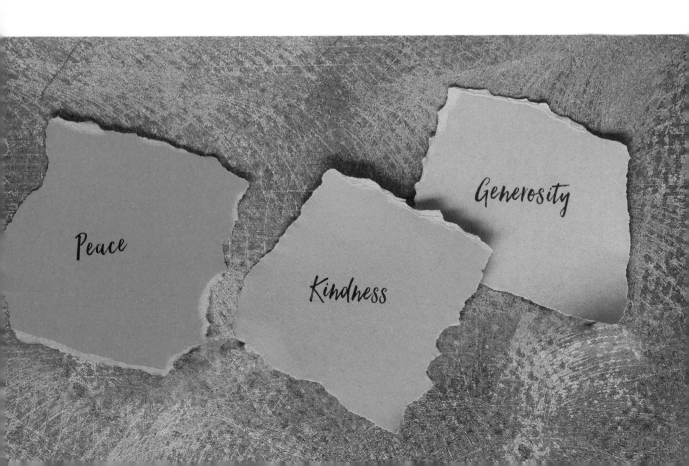

# BREAKFAST

After your morning routine, it's time to start the day with optimal energy and superfoods that will help you stay on top. Breakfast food should be a long-lasting source of energy while giving you a light feeling in your body. See what works best for you. For some, a smoothie is enough, while others need more solid energy, for example, a Love Bowl (see page 86). On weekends when you have more time, it can feel nice to give yourself that little extra; for example, Unicorn Toast and Breakfast Lollipops (see pages 85 and 89).

All these recipes can be combined and varied endlessly. Find your own favourites. When you feel confident with these recipes, you can start being creative and experimenting with different superfoods and ingredients.

*PS ...* *Just because you like coffee in the morning, it does not have to exclude a nutritious smoothie. You can always add health to the routines you already have.*

Crown Chakra

Third Eye Chakra

Throat Chakra

Heart Chakra

Solar Plexus Chakra

Sacral Chakra

Root Chakra

# CHAKRA SMOOTHIES

Smoothies are my favourite for breakfast because you can get so much nutrition in a single glass. Here you can combine many superfoods and ingredients that cover most of your daily needs in terms of minerals, antioxidants, good fats and vitamins. You can feel if the body needs more cleansing, replenishing, energizing or preventative effects.

It can take some time for the body to get used to an unfamiliar taste, so start with half a teaspoon if you choose superfoods with a strong taste and effect. After a few days, you can increase to a whole teaspoon, and about a week later you can follow the recommendation on the package.

You are often naturally drawn to a certain taste or colour during a period when you need these raw materials the most. If you have difficulty recognizing them, start with what feels most appealing at the moment and vary gradually. There is no right or wrong when you make a smoothie; use these basic recipes and then let your creativity flow.

**ALL RECIPES SERVE 1**

### ROOT CHAKRA
1 ripe banana
100g/3½oz frozen strawberries
250ml/9fl oz/1 cup plant-based milk
¼ teaspoon ground turmeric
¼ teaspoon ground ginger
¼ teaspoon ground cardamom
1 teaspoon maca powder
1 teaspoon cold-pressed coconut oil

> Mix everything thoroughly in a blender.

### SACRAL CHAKRA
200g/7oz frozen mango
100g/3½oz fresh or frozen papaya
300ml/10½fl oz/1¼ cups mixed carrot and
    orange juice (homemade or store-
    bought raw juice)
1 teaspoon rosehip powder

1 teaspoon camu camu powder
¼ teaspoon unsweetened vanilla powder

> Mix everything thoroughly in a blender.

### SOLAR PLEXUS CHAKRA
1 ripe banana
250ml/9fl oz/1 cup plant-based milk
100g/3½oz frozen mango
½ teaspoon ground cinnamon
½ teaspoon ground cardamom
½ teaspoon ground ginger
1 teaspoon baobab powder
¼ teaspoon vanilla powder
1 teaspoon cold-pressed coconut oil
¼ teaspoon agave syrup or coconut sugar

> Mix everything thoroughly in a blender.

### HEART CHAKRA
1 handful of kale
1 avocado
1 frozen ripe banana
½ teaspoon wheatgrass or barley grass
300ml/10½fl oz/1¼ cups almond milk
¼ teaspoon agave syrup or coconut
   sugar

> Mix everything thoroughly in
   a blender.

*PS* ...

*Wheatgrass and barley grass are filled with chlorophyll to oxygenate your blood, speed up circulation and help you clear out things you do not need. If you have a very sensitive stomach, I would recommend barley grass, which is slightly milder for the stomach than wheatgrass. Wonderful plant energy!*

### THROAT CHAKRA

1 large ripe banana
200ml/7fl oz/scant 1 cup
  plant-based milk
1 tablespoon tahini
1 tablespoon cold-pressed
  coconut oil
¼ teaspoon baobab
  powder
½ teaspoon unsweetened
  vanilla powder
1 pinch of liquorice powder
½ teaspoon blue spirulina
¼ teaspoon agave syrup or
  coconut sugar

> Mix everything
  thoroughly in a blender.

### THIRD EYE CHAKRA

200g/7oz frozen mango
1 handful of spinach
8 fresh mint leaves
250ml/9fl oz/1 cup plant-
  based milk
½ teaspoon blue spirulina
½ teaspoon agave syrup
  (optional)

> Mix everything
  thoroughly in a blender.

### CROWN CHAKRA

1 ripe banana
250ml/9fl oz/1 cup almond
  milk
100g/3½oz/¾ cup frozen
  blueberries
1 tablespoon peanut butter
1 teaspoon cold-pressed
  coconut oil
1 tablespoon acai powder
½ teaspoon ground
  cinnamon
1 teaspoon agave syrup
peel of ½ organic lemon

> Mix everything
  thoroughly in a blender.

*PS* ... *Spirulina powder has a high nutritional value and gives you high energy. It's suitable for the entire family! Get used to the taste slowly and gradually increase the amount until you can include up to 2 teaspoons in your smoothies.*

# CREATE YOUR OWN SMOOTHIE

Your smoothie can have every possible look, and you can experiment with different combinations. I usually stick to a base of plant-based milk and banana which I then build on with what I am craving or feel a need for.

   Of course, you can also make your smoothie with coconut water or fresh juices and replace the banana with avocado or frozen berries for a thicker texture. Here you get some suggestions on ingredients that you can add to your base. Try your hand at your own favourite combo!

**SERVES 1**

**BASIC SMOOTHIE**
1 large ripe banana
250ml/9fl oz/1 cup plant-based milk (oat milk,
    coconut milk, almond milk)

**CHOOSE YOUR INGREDIENTS**
Choose the ingredients that you think fit together:

100g/3½oz fresh or frozen berries
100g/3½oz fresh or frozen mango
100g/3½oz fresh or frozen papaya
1 handful of spinach
1 handful of kale
1 pinch of fresh mint leaves
peel of 1 organic lemon
peel of 1 organic lime
peel of 1 organic orange
1 teaspoon acai powder
1 teaspoon baobab powder
1 teaspoon camu camu powder
1 teaspoon wheatgrass or barley grass
½ teaspoon spirulina
½ teaspoon chlorella

1 tablespoon chia seeds
1 tablespoon cacao nibs
2 teaspoons raw cacao powder
1 tablespoon peanut butter
½ teaspoon unsweetened vanilla powder
½ teaspoon ground ginger
½ teaspoon ground turmeric
½ teaspoon ground cinnamon
½ teaspoon ground cardamom
1 teaspoon cold-pressed coconut oil
½ teaspoon coconut sugar
½ teaspoon agave syrup
2 Medjool dates, pitted
2 teaspoons agave syrup

*PS ...*    *For an extra energy boost in your smoothie, choose an ingredient from "Superfoods for an Extra Kick" (see page 91).*

Water

Salt flakes

Vanilla powder

Dates

Brazil nuts

Before I started making my own milks, I had a notion it was complicated and time-consuming, but it turned out to be so easy! Like so much else that you make yourself, it has a completely different taste compared to purchased, ready-made products. It is a wonderful way to get good nutrition, and this milk can also be varied endlessly. Do not be intimidated by the nut-milk bag. It is a one-time investment that is well worth every penny, and it quickly becomes your new friend in the kitchen. A wonderful awakening is promised!

## MAKES ABOUT 1L/35FL OZ/4¼ CUPS

### BASIC MILK
250g/9oz/2 cups raw nuts, soaked for at least 4 hours or overnight, then drained
1 teaspoon unsweetened vanilla powder
4 Medjool dates, pitted (or 1 tablespoon agave syrup)
¼ teaspoon sea salt flakes
1l/35fl oz/4¼ cups water (preferably filtered)

> Put the drained nuts, vanilla, dates, salt and 400ml/14fl oz/1⅔ cups of the water in a blender.
> Run at low speed for 3 minutes until the nuts have been ground down completely.
> Add the rest of the water and mix at high speed for another 3 minutes.
> Take a large bowl and thread your nut-milk bag over the edge.
> Pour everything from the blender into the bag and strain the milk.
> Squeeze out the remaining milk with your hands.
> Pour into a clean glass bottle and store in the refrigerator for a maximum of 2–3 days.

*PS ...*

*Super good for your smoothies or your porridge/oatmeal. Or just pour the milk over fresh berries or other superfoods. You can also use the seasonings for Rainbow Latte (see page 78) to create nutritious milk to take with you to work, or to enjoy in the evening.*

**Suggestions for nuts that you can use in the milk on the previous page.**

Brazil nuts

Macadamia nuts

Pecan nuts

PS ...

*Did you know that raw cacao has a vibration that opens the heart chakra? It is used worldwide in ancient cacao ceremonies. With its serotonin-enhancing properties, it also helps you to contact the third eye and a higher consciousness. So enjoy Mother Earth's natural "joy powder"!*

# QUICK NUT MILKS YOU CAN MAKE WITHOUT A NUT-MILK BAG

**BOTH RECIPES MAKE 1 BOTTLE**

**NOT WITHOUT MY COFFEE**
100g/3½oz/generous ¾ cup raw cashews
500ml/17fl oz/2 cups water
3 Medjool dates, pitted
¼ teaspoon unsweetened vanilla powder
¼ teaspoon sea salt flakes
1 espresso or decaf espresso

> Blitz the nuts in a blender to a flour.
> Add the rest of the ingredients and blend to mix well.
> Pour into a clean bottle.

**HIGH FREQUENCY**
100g/3½oz/generous ¾ cup raw cashews
500ml/17fl oz/2 cups water
2 Medjool dates, pitted
1 teaspoon raw cacao powder
1 teaspoon maca powder
¼ teaspoon unsweetened vanilla powder
¼ teaspoon sea salt flakes

> Blitz the nuts in a blender to a flour.
> Add the rest of the ingredients and blend to mix well.
> Pour into a clean bottle.

# HIGH-VIBE JUICE

Suitable for both centrifugal and cold pressed juicers. There will be no higher vibration than this!

**ALL RECIPES SERVE 1**

### GREEN LOVE
**RECIPE 1**
1 large handful of kale
1 pinch of fresh parsley leaves
1 large slice of organic lemon with peel
3 large red apples with peel
¼ teaspoon spirulina powder

> Start with the leaves, then add the lemon and apples.
> Finally, whisk the spirulina into your juice.

**RECIPE 2**
1 handful of kale
1 handful of spinach leaves
1 medium celery stalk
1cm/½in piece of fresh ginger
1 large slice of organic lemon with peel
2 large red apples with peel
¼ teaspoon wheatgrass powder

> Start with the leaves, then add the celery, ginger, lemon and apples.
> Finally, whisk the wheatgrass into your juice.

### ORANGE POWER
**RECIPE 1**
2 large carrots
1 slice of organic lemon with peel
2cm/¾in piece of fresh ginger
5cm/2in piece of fresh turmeric, unpeeled
3cm/1¼in piece of fresh red chilli, deseeded
2 large red apples with peel

> Squeeze all the ingredients.

**RECIPE 2**
2 large carrots
2 large oranges, peeled
1 small, whole organic lemon
1cm/½in piece of fresh ginger
½ teaspoon baobab powder
¼ teaspoon unsweetened vanilla powder

> Squeeze the carrots, oranges, lemon and ginger.
> Finally, whisk the baobab and vanilla powders into your juice.

### ROOT YOURSELF
**RECIPE 1**
1 large handful of spinach leaves
1 medium beetroot/beet
1 segment of lime with peel
2 large red apples with peel

> Start with the spinach leaves. Then squeeze the beetroot/beet, lime and apples.

**RECIPE 2**
2 medium beetroots/beets
1 large celery stalk
2 large pears, unpeeled
1 kiwi, peeled
1cm/½in piece of fresh ginger
1 large pinch of fresh mint

> Juice all the ingredients.

*PS ...*

*Juicing is the best way I know to make the whole body vibrate with energy. My favourites are the green ones. Once you get used to drinking your vegetables, you can increase the amount of leaves and celery a little at a time. If you feel juices are your thing, I highly recommend you buy a cold-press juicer. It is a small investment, but you get at least twice the amount of juice – all liquid from the green leaves – and the juice keeps for up to 3 days in the refrigerator (so you can make a batch for the start of your week and pour into bottles that you can take with you).*

*A centrifugal juicer is still a great alternative to the juices bought in stores. Preferably drink the juice from a centrifugal juicer within a few hours to maintain the nutritional value. You can also turn your green juices into a smoothie by pouring them into your blender along with frozen banana and avocado.*

# RAINBOW LATTE

Try replacing or varying your regular latte with these colourful and nutritious versions. Also good to enjoy in the evening as a hot drink before bed.

**SERVES 1**

**WHEATGRASS LATTE**
1 teaspoon wheatgrass powder
¼ teaspoon ground ginger
¼ teaspoon ground cardamom
200ml/7fl oz/scant 1 cup almond milk or other plant-based barista milk, preferably skimmed
½ teaspoon agave syrup

> Mix together the wheatgrass, ginger and cardamom.
> Heat the milk on low until it becomes lukewarm.
> Add a little milk to the powder mixture and stir well.
> Stir in the agave syrup.
> Top up with the rest of the warm milk.

**SERVES 1**

### RASPBERRY LATTE

1 tablespoon freeze-dried raspberry
   powder
¼ teaspoon unsweetened vanilla powder
¼ teaspoon maca powder
200ml/7fl oz/scant 1 cup plant-based milk,
   preferably frothy
1 teaspoon agave syrup

> Mix the powders together.
> Heat the milk on low until lukewarm.
> Add a little milk to the powder mixture
   and stir well.
> Stir in the agave syrup.
> Top up with the rest of the warm milk.

Cardamom

Ginger

Vanilla powder

Turmeric

Cinnamon

**SERVES 1**

### TURMERIC LATTE
½ teaspoon ground turmeric
½ teaspoon ground cinnamon
1 pinch of ground cardamom
½ teaspoon ground ginger
¼ teaspoon unsweetened vanilla
  powder
200ml/7fl oz/scant 1 cup plant-based
  milk, preferably frothy
½ teaspoon agave syrup

> Mix together the ground spices and vanilla powder.
> Skim the milk and heat on low until lukewarm.
> Add a little milk to the powder mixture and stir well.
> Stir in the agave syrup.
> Top up with the rest of the warm milk.

# BLUE SMURF LATTE

**SERVES 1**

½ teaspoon blue spirulina powder
¼ teaspoon unsweetened vanilla powder
¼ teaspoon ground cardamom
200ml/7fl oz/scant 1 cup almond milk or
barrista oatmilk, preferably skimmed
½ teaspoon agave syrup

> Mix together the spirulina, vanilla and
  cardamom.
> Skim the plant-based milk and heat on low
  until it becomes lukewarm.
> Add a little milk to the powder mixture and
  stir well.
> Stir in the agave syrup.
> Top up with the rest of the warm milk.

*PS ...*

*Blue spirulina has become a big trend in
the health world. It is actually the blue
component of the regular spirulina that
has been separated from the green. You
can find blue spirulina in online stores
and well-stocked health-food stores.*

# UNICORN TOAST

## SERVES 1

1 tablespoon each of pink, yellow and blue
   pastel spread (see right)
1 slice of banana bread (see below), preferably
   toasted
fresh blueberries

> Spread the pastel mixtures in three parts over
  the banana bread.
> Top with blueberries.

### BANANA BREAD
500g/1lb 2oz porridge/rolled oats
75g/2½oz/½ cup cornflour/cornstarch
1 teaspoon bicarbonate of soda/baking soda
1½ tablespoons ground cinnamon
3 tablespoons grated coconut
½ teaspoon sea salt flakes
2 large ripe bananas, chopped into small pieces
2 tablespoons cold-pressed coconut oil, melted
1 tablespoon agave syrup
200g/7oz/1 cup oat yogurt with vanilla flavour or
   any plant-based yogurt
200g/7oz/2 cups coarsely chopped pecans
   (optional)

> Preheat the oven to 180°C/350°F/gas 4.
> Blitz the porridge/rolled oats into a flour
  in a food processor.
> Add all the remaining dry ingredients and
  mix them together.

> Add the bananas, coconut oil, agave syrup and
  yogurt.
> Mix into a batter and stir in the pecans, if using.
> Grease a rectangular loaf pan with a little extra
  coconut oil and pour in the batter.
> Bake in the middle of the oven for 25 minutes,
  or until the surface has a nice colour.
> Let it cool before slicing.

### PASTEL SPREAD
200g/7oz/scant 1 cup tofu spread (or other plant-
   based cream cheese)
zest of 1 organic lemon and 2 tablespoons freshly
   squeezed juice
1 tablespoon agave syrup

> Mix all the ingredients thoroughly with a
  balloon whisk.
> Divide the mixture into 3 bowls.

### PINK MIXTURE
> Mix the base with a little freeze-dried raspberry
  powder for the desired colour.

### YELLOW MIXTURE
> Mix the base with a little freeze-dried passion
  fruit powder for the desired colour.

### BLUE MIXTURE
> Mix the base with a little blue spirulina powder
  for the desired colour.

*PS ...*

*In health-food stores, well-stocked supermarkets and on the internet,
you will find freeze-dried fruits and berry powders. They contain a lot of
nutrients and can be used for all your breakfast favourites.*
   *The banana bread is insanely good and we also eat it with peanut butter
or just as hot toast with a little coconut oil on it. For dinner, you can serve
it with a Bliss Bowl (see page 118), or with Orange Hummus (see page 96).
Yummy!*

# LOVE BOWLS

**ALL RECIPES SERVE 1**

**PURPLE DREAM**
1 large ripe frozen banana
100g/3½oz/¾ cup frozen strawberries
100g/3½oz/¾ cup frozen blueberries
1 tablespoon acai powder
½ teaspoon ground cinnamon
1 teaspoon agave syrup or coconut sugar

> Blitz everything thoroughly in a blender or
  food processor, then top with some optional
  toppings (see right).

**GREEN FAVOURITE**
1 handful of spinach leaves
1 large ripe frozen banana
200g/7oz frozen mango
10 fresh mint leaves
3 tablespoons plant-based milk, preferably
  sweetened
1 tablespoon grated coconut
1 teaspoon hemp seeds, hulled (optional)
¼ teaspoon spirulina powder

> Blitz everything thoroughly in a blender or
  food processor, then top with some optional
  toppings (see right).

**SUNSHINE**
1 large ripe frozen banana
200g/7oz frozen mango
3 tablespoons frozen raspberries
½ teaspoon unsweetened vanilla powder
1 teaspoon baobab powder
grated zest of 1 organic lemon

> Blitz everything thoroughly in a blender or
  food processor, then top with some optional
  toppings (see right).

**CHOOSE YOUR TOPPINGS**
apple wedges
banana slices
blackberries
blueberries
kiwi
mango
melon
passion fruit
raspberries
strawberries
Salty Cacao Granola (see page 89)
a dollop of Almond Butter with Pecan and
  Vanilla (see page 89) or peanut butter
coconut flakes or grated coconut
optional nuts
hemp seeds
pumpkin seeds
sunflower seeds
edible flowers

# BREAKFAST LOLLIPOPS

## MAKES 5 LOLLIPOPS

1 ripe, firm banana, halved widthways
Almond Butter with Pecan and Vanilla (see below;
   store-bought peanut butter also works well)
salty cacao granola (see below)
wooden lollipop sticks

> Take the banana halves and push the wooden
  stick in the wider part so you get a lollipop
  (see picture). Spread the almond butter over
  the banana and then roll it in the granola.
> Serve immediately.

## ALMOND BUTTER WITH PECAN AND VANILLA

200g/7oz/1½ cups whole raw almonds
100g/3½oz/1 cup raw pecans
3½ tablespoons cold-pressed coconut oil, melted
½ teaspoon unsweetened vanilla powder
1 tablespoon maple syrup
1 teaspoon sea salt flakes

> Blitz everything in a food processor until you
  get a creamy mixture, stopping frequently
  to scrape down the sides – it takes up to 10
  minutes.
> Store in a tightly closed jar at room
  temperature.

## SALTY CACAO GRANOLA

500g/1lb 2oz/5 cups gluten-free porridge/
rolled oats
300g/10½oz/3 cups raw pecans, coarsely
   chopped
200g/7oz/1¼ cups pumpkin seeds
100g/3½oz/¾ cup sesame seeds, hulled
200g/7oz/4 cups coconut flakes
100g/3½oz/generous ¾ cup cacao nibs
10 Medjool dates, pitted and coarsely chopped
3 tablespoons cold-pressed coconut oil
4 tablespoons raw cacao powder
2 teaspoons unsweetened vanilla powder
4 tablespoons agave syrup
½ teaspoon sea salt flakes

> Mix the oats, nuts, seeds, coconut flakes, cacao
  nibs and dates in a large bowl.
> Gently melt the coconut oil in a small pan to a
  maximum of 37°C/99°F, then stir in the cacao
  and vanilla powders and the agave syrup.
> Add the oat mixture and stir well to mix.
> Crumble in the salt flakes and stir again.
> Preheat the oven to 50°C/120°F/gas ¼. Spread
  the granola mixture on a baking sheet lined
  with baking parchment and bake for 3–4 hours,
  depending on your oven. Open a small gap in
  the oven door from time to time.

*PS ...*

*At home I make a large batch of both granola and almond butter and
store them in large jars. I top my love bowls, morning porridge/oatmeal
and chia puddings with granola. It is also good on a simple fruit salad or
with a little coconut yogurt. My favourite!*

*You can spread the almond butter on your corn cakes, top porridge
with it, or spread it on tropical fruit.*

*I usually freeze breakfast lollipops and turn them into ice cream sticks
for the kids!*

# CHAKRA FOODS FOR THE DAY

This section contains a selection of the dishes that are regularly cooked in my family. They are simple, filling and really tasty. These recipes are meant as a foundation that you can then build on. Once you have tasted the dishes, you can combine them to suit your taste, and also create new dishes from this base. That's when it's fun!

The Energizing Food recipes will help boost your energy in a colourful way, and the Grounding Food recipes are soul filling and give your energy comfort. The Natural Desserts From Mother Earth chapter provides sweet and colourful food to boost positivity, and the Liquid Balance chapter shows how you can infuse your water to cleanse your body and bring more flow into your life.

All of the recipes are suitable for all occasions – lunch, dinner, a quick weekday meal or even to serve party guests. At home, I love to have a lot of small dishes with different dips, sauces and stir-fries. It's a more fun way to experience your food, and the different flavour combinations keep it varied. It's easier than you think, and the feeling afterwards is uplifting!

# SUPERFOODS FOR AN EXTRA ENERGY KICK

I am very fond of superfood powder. It is like absorbing vibrating plant intelligence directly into the body, where every leaf, grass, berry, fungus, root and herb refuels the body. Once you have learned to find the right one in the wide range and tried it out, it is possible to get an enormous amount of nutrition and energy from these powders. The reason they are called superfoods is that they have such a high nutrient content compressed in a small amount of powder.

Often 1–2 teaspoons are enough to get the right effect. They are prepared by gentle drying at a low temperature or freeze-drying, to keep as much of the nutrient content as possible. Many of these superfoods have been used by indigenous peoples around the world for thousands of years.

They were used in Chinese medicine, Indian Ayurveda, but also by the Aztecs, in the Andes and the Amazon. It is amazing that even we in the western world can now partake of this ancient wisdom from nature! There are many superfoods that I have used in the book and they all have unique properties. The selection in this chapter increases your energy, makes you alert and focused, and strengthens your immune system a little more.

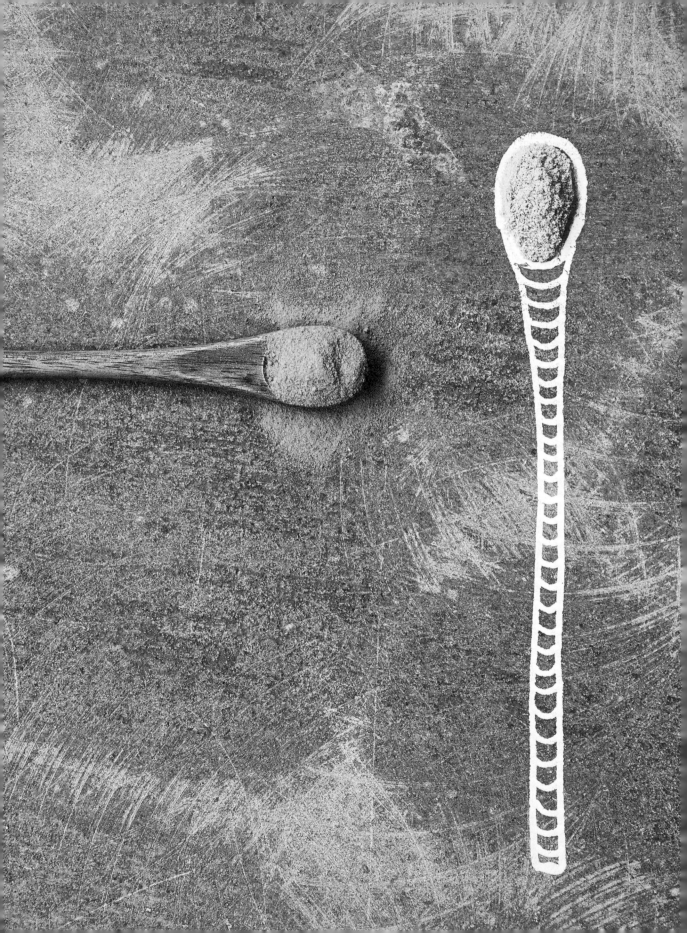

## MACA

Maca is a superfood from the Incas. It increases vital energy and balances your hormones, as well as reducing physical and mental stress. It clears away negative energy and gives you greater mental clarity and a stronger immune system.

## GUARANA

Guarana comes from the Amazon and Brazil. It contains more caffeine than coffee and you get long-lasting energy but without the acidifying effect of coffee. It's good to eat in the morning, after lunch or before training when you need a more focused energy. It also contains a lot of antioxidants.

## REISHI

Reishi is a fungus used in Chinese medicine. It builds life force and strengthens your energy and heart. It cleanses the liver and thus clears away heavy old energy.

## CHAGA

Chaga grows on birch trees. It contains high levels of antioxidants and has an ability to increase oxygen uptake in the body. Chaga builds new energy for longer endurance. It is highly anti-inflammatory and helps the body to heal itself.

## CORDYCEPS

Cordyceps is a Chinese mushroom from the Himalayas that builds up energy and increases the body's physical strength and performance ability. It reduces mental fatigue and helps the body stay healthy, especially during cold times. The fungus is also good for the kidneys, bladder and heart.

## GINSENG

The Chinese root ginseng balances blood sugar and keeps your mood in balance. It reduces stress and provides energy. Ginseng is also said to slow down ageing and give new vitality.

## TURMERIC

Turmeric has an anti-inflammatory effect and cleanses the blood. It is a powerful antioxidant that has been used in Indian Ayurveda through the ages. Turmeric is also considered to slow down ageing.

## SCHISANDRA

A Chinese berry used in Chinese medicine, schisandra reduces stress and chronic fatigue, strengthens your heart and your mental health and balances the body. The berry also cleanses your liver and kidneys, increases your blood circulation and gives vitality.

*PS ...*

*Avoid these superfoods if you are pregnant or breastfeeding, so you do not disturb your baby's energy. Good superfoods for you and your baby are instead raspberries, strawberries, blueberries, acai, baobab, camu camu and spirulina. The same goes for younger children.*

# ENERGIZING FOOD

Honour your body with colourful and nourishing foods. Here you give all your chakras a boost to keep a balance. When you eat all the colours of the rainbow, you can be sure that you get a variety of nutrition and at the same time the energy you need to be your own healer. Different tastes and textures gives your body a satisfying feeling after your meal.

Explore, enjoy and give blessing to your wonderful meals. Let it be an explosion of vibrant healing foods in a playful form. Eat the rainbow!

# THREE KINDS OF HUMMUS

Three wonderful dips to eat any time, whether it's a weekday or a party. Serve as a snack with beetroot/beet chips or add a spoonful with your salads. I usually put a spoonful in our wraps and on our corn cakes or gluten-free bread, or use it as a dip for vegetables.

**SERVES 2–4**

**GREEN**

300g/10½oz/2½ cups frozen green peas, defrosted
100g/3½oz/¾ cup canned chickpeas/ garbanzo beans, rinsed and drained
3½ tablespoons extra virgin olive oil
½ garlic clove, peeled
1 hearty pinch of fresh mint
1 teaspoon freshly squeezed lemon juice
1 large pinch of sea salt flakes
a few grinds of black pepper

> Blitz everything in a food processor to a smooth consistency.

**RED**

300g/10½oz/2 cups canned chickpeas/ garbanzo beans, rinsed and drained
1 large cooked beetroot/beet
3½ tablespoons extra virgin olive oil
1 teaspoon ground cumin
4 teaspoons freshly squeezed lemon juice
1 large pinch of sea salt flakes
a few grinds of black pepper

> Blitz everything in a food processor to a smooth consistency.

**ORANGE**

1 large sweet potato, peeled, diced and cooked
200g/7oz/1½ cups canned chickpeas/ garbanzo beans, rinsed and drained
3½ tablespoons extra virgin olive oil
2 teaspoons freshly squeezed lemon or orange juice
¼ teaspoon ground turmeric
¼ teaspoon chilli powder
¼ teaspoon smoked paprika
½ teaspoon dried rosemary
½ garlic clove, peeled
1 large pinch of sea salt flakes
a few grinds of black pepper

> Blitz everything in a food processor to a smooth consistency.

# COLOURFUL CANAPÉS

### SERVES 2–4

1 package mini corn or rice cakes (available in
     well-stocked supermarkets and health-food stores)
pink, yellow and blue pastel spreads (see page 85)

> Mash each pastel mixture (pink, yellow and
  blue).
> Spread thickly on the mini corn cakes and
  decorate with the optional toppings below.

### CHOOSE YOUR TOPPINGS
fresh blueberries
fresh figs
fresh mint leaves
fresh physalis/Cape gooseberry
fresh raspberries
fresh strawberries

# SUPER SIMPLE RAW TOMATO SAUCE

**SERVES 2–4**

5 large ripe tomatoes, cut into large wedges
50g/1¾oz sun-dried tomatoes in oil
1 medium celery stalk, chopped
1 garlic clove, crushed
2 tablespoons extra virgin olive oil
2 tablespoons fresh basil
1 teaspoon sea salt flakes
a few grinds of black pepper

> Blitz everything roughly in a food processor.
> Serve with courgette/zucchini spaghetti or cooked gluten-free pasta.

*PS ...*

*Replace the basil with fresh coriander/cilantro and use in your tacos, nachos or as a dip on the table. You can also stir Raw Walnut Mince (see page 117) into the tomato sauce and serve as a raw Bolognese, or eat it with the Courgette Swirl with Citrus and Pumpkin Seed Pesto (see page 103), or add small salad leaves with Guacamole and Raw Walnut Mince (see pages 104 and 117).*

# COURGETTE SWIRL WITH CITRUS AND PUMPKIN SEED PESTO

### SERVES 2–4

2 medium courgettes/zucchini, spiralized
1 batch Citrus and Pumpkin Seed Pesto
(see below)
12–15 cherry tomatoes, halved
sea salt flakes and freshly ground black pepper

> Mix the courgettes/zucchini with the pesto
  in a large bowl.
> Sprinkle over the tomato halves and season
  to taste.

### CITRUS AND PUMPKIN SEED PESTO
100g/3½oz/¾ cup raw pumpkin seeds
100ml/3½fl oz/scant ½ cup extra virgin olive oil
grated zest of 1 organic lemon
4 tablespoons freshly squeezed lemon juice
1 small garlic clove, peeled
100g/3½oz fresh basil or lemon balm
1 teaspoon sea salt flakes
a few grinds of black pepper

> Blitz everything in a food processor until smooth.

# ROASTED MULTICOLOUR ROOT VEGETABLES WITH GUACAMOLE

**SERVES 2–4**

1 large sweet potato
3 beetroots/beets
3 Chioggia beetroots/beets
2 tablespoons extra virgin olive oil, plus extra
   for greasing
1 pinch of sea salt flakes
1 pinch of fresh coriander/cilantro

> Preheat the oven to 250°C/500°F/gas 9.
> Cut all the vegetables into medium-thick
   wedges.
> Grease a large baking sheet and lay out the
   wedges so that they are separate from each
   other.
> Roast for 20–25 minutes, or until the vegetables
   have softened but still have some bite.
> Allow to cool slightly, then drizzle with the
   olive oil and sprinkle with the salt and
   coriander/cilantro.

**GUACAMOLE**

2 large ripe avocados
1 tablespoon extra virgin olive oil
1 teaspoon freshly squeezed lime juice
1 hearty pinch of fresh coriander/cilantro,
   coarsely chopped
sea salt flakes and freshly ground black pepper,
   to taste

> Mash everything together with a fork to a
   creamy texture.

*PS ...*

*I put this guacamole on everything! On corn cakes, on toasted gluten-free bread topped with chilli flakes, on my bliss bowls... and I also dip my nachos in it. I love avocados, which give the heart chakra the right energy for the day!*

# CABBAGE LEAF WRAPS WITH MANGO AND TAHINI DIP

**SERVES 2–4**

**IN EACH CABBAGE LEAF**
**(1 CABBAGE LEAF PER PORTION):**
2 tablespoons Tahini dDp (see right), stirred
2 tablespoons shredded red cabbage
2 tablespoons coarsely grated carrot
4–6 cubes of mango
3 thin slices of honeydew melon, peeled
4 slices of a deseeded red pepper

> Spread a thick line of tahini in the middle of each cabbage leaf.
> Sprinkle the red cabbage and carrot on top of the tahini.
> Add the mango, melon and red pepper, evenly distributed, and fold up each cabbage leaf like a spring roll (fold in the edges, then the bottom and roll up all the way).
> Cut in half with a sharp knife and serve with a small bowl of Tahini Dip (see right).

**TAHINI DIP**
100g/3½oz/½ cup tahini
3 tablespoons freshly squeezed lime juice
5 tablespoons agave syrup
1 teaspoon sea salt flakes
3½ tablespoons water

> Place everything in a food processor and blitz until smooth.

# RAMEN

### SERVES 2–4

1 large handful of spinach leaves
1 large handful of courgette/zucchini, spiralized
1 handful of julienned carrot
1 handful of shredded red cabbage
1 handful of fresh bean sprouts
hot Ginger Broth (see below)
roasted salted cashews, coarsely chopped
fresh coriander/cilantro

> Put all the vegetables in each bowl.
> Pour over the hot ginger broth.
> Top with roasted cashews and coriander/cilantro.

### GINGER BROTH
5cm/2in piece of fresh ginger, grated
3 large garlic cloves, grated
¼ teaspoon chilli flakes
1 tablespoon cold-pressed coconut oil
1.5l/52fl oz/6½ cups water
3 tablespoons vegetable stock/bouillon powder
freshly squeezed juice of 1 lime
1 tablespoon agave syrup
Sea salt to taste

> Sweat the ginger, garlic and chilli flakes in the
  coconut oil without letting them colour.
> Pour over the water and stock, bring to the boil
  and simmer for 10–15 minutes.
> Strain the broth.
> Finish with the lime juice and agave syrup.

*PS ...*

*You can also top the soup with a little tofu or
Quorn pieces fried in soy sauce, if you want
a little variety.*

# ASIAN VEGGIE BURGERS IN CABBAGE LEAF WRAP WITH HOT PLUM DIP

**SERVES 2–4**

**IN EACH CABBAGE LEAF
(1 CABBAGE LEAF PER PORTION):**
1 handful of julienned courgette/zucchini
1 handful of julienned carrot
3 Veggie Burgers (see below)
1 tablespoon fresh coriander/cilantro

**TO SERVE**
1 generous handful of pea shoots

> Put the courgette/zucchini and carrot in the bottom of your cabbage leaf.
> Then place 3 small burgers on top of the vegetables.
> Top with the fresh coriander/cilantro and tie the wrap together with natural string (see picture).
> Serve with a generous handful of pea shoots and the Hot Plum Dip (see right).

**VEGGIE BURGERS**
200g/7oz/1½ cups canned chickpeas/garbanzo beans, rinsed and drained
½ medium sweet potato, peeled and coarsely grated
1 red chilli, deseeded and chopped
2cm/¾in piece of fresh ginger, finely grated
½ garlic clove, crushed
1 small handful of fresh coriander/cilantro
freshly squeezed juice of 1 lime
100g/3½oz/2/3 cup cornflour/cornstarch
1 tablespoon grated coconut
1 teaspoon cold-pressed coconut oil, plus extra for frying
1 teaspoon sea salt flakes
1 teaspoon agave syrup

> Blitz everything in a food processor until fully combined.
> Shape the mixture into small, flat round patties.
> Heat a little coconut oil in a frying pan over a medium heat and fry the patties until golden brown.

**HOT PLUM DIP**
100g/3½oz/scant ½ cup Asian hot plum sauce (available in Asian stores as well as in well-stocked supermarkets)
3½ tablespoons tamari soy sauce
2cm/¾in piece of fresh ginger, finely grated

> Stir the ingredients together well.
> Serve in small bowls or glasses.

*PS ...*    *It's good to sprinkle some chopped, salty cashews in the Hot Plum Dip (see above). As an alternative to the Veggie Burgers above, serve it with Roasted Multicolour Root Vegetables with Guacamole (see page 104), or just a cup of Ginger Broth from the Ramen recipe on page 109.*

# RAINBOW BURGERS

## MAKES 4, 1-CABBAGE LEAF WRAP PER PERSON

### IN EACH LARGE RED CABBAGE LEAF:
1 handful of coarsely shredded cos/romaine lettuce
1 Beetroot/beet Burger (see below)
2–3 tablespoons Curry Mix (see right)
5–7 Pickled Red Onion Rings (see right)
4 slices of nectarine, peach or persimmon (depending on season)
1 pinch of fresh thyme
edible purple flowers such as cornflowers and lilac

> Bend the red cabbage leaf in the middle so you get one bottom and a "lid".
> Place a thin bed of lettuce in the bottom of the cabbage leaf.
> Place the beetroot/beet burger on top of the salad.
> Drizzle the curry mix over the burger and top with the Pickled Red Onion Rings.
> Place slices of fruit on top and sprinkle over some thyme and flowers.

### BEETROOT/BEET BURGERS
120g/4½oz/1 cup pumpkin seeds
130g/4½oz beetroot/beet, finely grated
400g/14oz can chickpeas/garbanzo beans, rinsed and drained
400g/14oz can black beans, rinsed and drained
½ red onion
50g/1¾oz fresh thyme
1 teaspoon paprika
¼ teaspoon cayenne pepper
5 teaspoons extra virgin olive oil

¼ teaspoon natural smoke aroma (available in well-stocked supermarkets) or ½ teaspoon smoked paprika
1 teaspoon sea salt flakes
a few grinds of black pepper

> Grind the pumpkin seeds to a flour in a food processor.
> Blitz all the remaining ingredients together with the pumpkin seed flour in a food processor to make a coarse mixture.
> Divide into 4 burgers.

### CURRY MIX
200g/7oz/scant 1 cup oat fraîche (or other plant-based crème fraîche)
2 tablespoons yellow curry powder
1 teaspoon apple cider vinegar
1 tablespoon extra virgin olive oil
2 tablespoons agave syrup
½ teaspoon sea salt flakes

> Mix together all the ingredients with a balloon whisk.

### PICKLED RED ONION RINGS
100ml/3½fl oz/scant ½ cup apple cider vinegar
200ml/7fl oz/scant 1 cup water
100ml/3½fl oz/scant ½ cup agave syrup
3 star anise
4 red onions, cut into thin rings

> Mix together the vinegar, water and agave syrup in a large, clean screw-top jar.
> Add the star anise and onion rings, seal the lid and leave to marinate for at least 1 hour.
> Store in the sealed jar and keep for up to 5 days in the refrigerator.

*PS ...*

*We often eat this type of food as a self-serve meal, placing bowls with the various accompaniments on the dining table and letting everyone build their own burger. Nice and relaxed!*

# FRESH VIETNAMESE ROLLS WITH DIP

**SERVES 2–4**

**IN EACH RICE PAPER (1 RICE PAPER PER PORTION):**
4 thin slices of kiwi, strawberry or mango
5 sugar snap peas, chopped
4 slices of deseeded red pepper
5 carrot sticks, julienne
1 tablespoon finely shredded red cabbage
2 tablespoons thin rice noodles, cooked al dente
1 tablespoon fresh bean sprouts
1 tablespoon roasted cashews or peanuts,
   coarsely chopped
1 tablespoon fresh coriander/cilantro

> Soak the rice paper in water and place on
  a plate.
> Place a row of any fruit down the middle of
  the paper.
> Sprinkle the sugar snap peas, red pepper,
  carrot and red cabbage over the fruit.
> Add a row of rice noodles and top everything
  with the bean sprouts, nuts and coriander/
  cilantro.
> Fold in the side edges first, then the bottom
  and roll everything into a spring roll.
> Serve with both dips (see right) in small bowls.

**FANTASTIC DIP**
1 tablespoon sesame seeds
100ml/3½fl oz/scant ½ cup tamari soy sauce
100ml/3½fl oz/scant ½ cup agave syrup
1 tablespoon toasted sesame oil
1 tablespoon rice vinegar
1 pinch of cayenne pepper

> Toast the sesame seeds in a dry frying pan
  over a low heat until slightly browned. Keep
  an eye out so they do not burn!
> Stir together the tamari soy and syrup until
  well blended.
> Pour in the rest of the ingredients and mix well.

**RASPBERRY AND TAHINI DIP**
50g/1¾oz/¼ cup tahini
2 teaspoons tamari soy sauce
1 teaspoon coconut milk
freshly squeezed juice of 1 lime
2 tablespoons agave syrup
2 teaspoons freeze-dried raspberry powder
½ teaspoon toasted sesame oil
3½ tablespoons water

> Blitz all the ingredients in a food processor
  or blender until smooth.

# MINI TACOS WITH WALNUTS, GUACAMOLE AND MANGO

**SERVES 2–4**

**IN EACH MINI TORTILLA (GLUTEN-FREE):**
1 handful of shredded cos/romaine lettuce
50g/3½oz Raw Walnut Mince (see right)
1 handful of finely shredded red cabbage
1 handful of spiralized courgette/zucchini
1 handful of spiralized carrot
1 tablespoon Guacamole (see page 104)
3 tablespoons mango pieces, fresh or frozen and defrosted
1 tablespoon frozen sweetcorn/corn kernels, defrosted, or fresh
1 teaspoon fresh coriander/cilantro

> Sprinkle the lettuce diagonally over the mini tortilla.
> Place the walnut mince on top of the lettuce.

> Sprinkle the red cabbage, courgette/zucchini and carrot on top of the walnut mince.
> Spoon the guacamole on top of everything and sprinkle with the mango and sweetcorn/corn kernels.
> Top with the fresh coriander/cilantro.

**RAW WALNUT MINCE**
200g/7oz/2 cups raw walnuts
1 tablespoon tamari soy sauce
1 tablespoon ground coriander
1 tablespoon ground cumin
½ teaspoon paprika
½ red pepper, deseeded
1 garlic clove, crushed
½ teaspoon sea salt flakes

> Blitz everything in a food processor to a coarse minced-/ground-meat consistency.

*PS ...*

*It's nice to serve mini tacos on a large chopping/cutting board or on baking parchment directly on the table so everyone can scoop their own. But it's also great if everyone can make their own tacos right at the table, in which case you can just display all the accompaniments in bowls.*

*Raw walnut mince is a firm favourite that also goes well with cooked gluten-free pasta, nachos, salad, or on gluten-free pizzas.*

# BLISS BOWL WITH RED CINNAMON RICE, COLESLAW WITH ORANGE, CHICKPEA BALLS AND FIGS

**SERVES 2–4**

**IN EACH BOWL:**
2 large cos/romaine lettuce leaves
1 handful of spinach leaves
100g/3½oz/¾ cup Red Cinnamon Rice (see below)
2 tablespoons Red Coleslaw with Orange
  (see right)
5 Chickpea Balls (see right)
1 fresh fig, halved
3 slices of orange
6 whole walnuts
1 handful of pea shoots
extra virgin olive oil, to drizzle
sea salt flakes and freshly ground black pepper

> Add the lettuce to the bowl so that the leaves protrude (see picture).
> Sprinkle the spinach leaves in the bottom of the bowl.
> Place a pile of rice on one side and a pile of coleslaw on the other.
> Place the chickpea balls in a pile next to the coleslaw and put the fig halves on the side.
> Add the orange slices and sprinkle with the nuts.
> Form a small ball of pea shoots and place next to the rice.
> Drizzle over a little olive oil. Season to taste.

**RED CINNAMON RICE**
1 tablespoon cold-pressed coconut oil
300g/10½oz/1½ cups red rice
1 tablespoon vegetable stock/bouillon powder
600ml/21fl oz/2½ cups water
1 tablespoon ground cinnamon

> Heat the coconut oil in a heavy saucepan over a medium-high heat.
> Fry the red rice in the oil and sprinkle over the stock/bouillon powder.
> Pour in the water, bring to the boil and cook the rice according to the instructions on the package.
> Allow to cool, then finally stir in the cinnamon.

**RED COLESLAW WITH ORANGE**
200g/7oz/¾ cup oat fraîche (or other plant-based crème fraîche)
grated zest of 1 large organic orange
1 tablespoon extra virgin olive oil
1 small garlic clove, crushed
½ teaspoon sea salt flakes
½ teaspoon freshly ground black pepper
1 pinch of cayenne pepper
100g/3½oz red cabbage, finely shredded

> Whisk together everything except the red cabbage and then stir through the cabbage just before serving.

**CHICKPEA BALLS**
200g/7oz/1½ cups canned chickpeas/garbanzo beans, rinsed and drained
½ sweet potato, peeled and coarsely grated
½ medium celery stalk, chopped
1 garlic clove, peeled
½ teaspoon dried oregano
½ teaspoon ground cinnamon
½ teaspoon ground cumin
2 pinches of cayenne pepper
1 tablespoon freshly squeezed lemon juice
1 tablespoon extra virgin olive oil, plus extra for frying
100g/3½oz/2/3 cup cornflour/cornstarch
1 teaspoon sea salt flakes
a few grinds of black pepper

> Blitz everything in your food processor to a smooth mixture.
> Divide into small balls.
> Fry in olive oil over a medium heat until golden brown.

# BLISS BOWL WITH KALE, HAZELNUT PESTO, BEETROOT BALLS AND CINNAMON APPLES

**SERVES 2–4**

**IN EACH BOWL:**
2 large cos/romaine lettuce leaves
1 red cabbage leaf
1 handful of spiralized courgette/zucchini
100g/3½oz Stir-fried Kale (see below)
2 tablespoons Hazelnut Pesto (see right)
4–6 Beetroot/beet Balls (see right)
8 thin slices of red apple dusted with ground
   cinnamon
6–7 Pickled Red Onion Rings (see page 113)
½ avocado, sliced
1 teaspoon sesame seeds
extra virgin olive oil, to drizzle
sea salt flakes and freshly ground black pepper

> Place the lettuce and red cabbage leaves in the bottom of the bowl.
> Put the courgette/zucchini on the side.
> Add a pile of stir-fried kale and hazelnut pesto, followed by the beetroot/beet balls and slices of cinnamon-dusted apples.
> Top with the pickled red onion rings and avocado slices and sprinkle with the sesame seeds.
> Drizzle over a little olive oil. Season to taste.

**STIR-FRIED KALE**
1 tablespoon extra virgin olive oil
1 large garlic clove, finely sliced
200g/7oz kale, coarsely chopped
½ teaspoon sea salt flakes

> Heat a frying pan over a medium heat.
> Pour in the olive oil and let the garlic sweat a little in it without getting colour.
> Put in the kale and let it soften and collapse slightly.
> Add the salt, turn the kale over and remove from the heat.

**HAZELNUT PESTO**
300g/10½oz/2¼ cups raw hazelnuts
100ml/3½fl oz/scant ½ cup extra virgin olive oil
grated zest of 1 organic lemon
1 tablespoon freshly squeezed lemon juice
1 large handful of fresh basil
1 teaspoon sea salt flakes
freshly ground black pepper, to taste

> Blitz everything in a food processor, pulsing to a coarse pesto.

**BEETROOT/BEET BALLS**
> Follow the recipe for the beetroot/beet Burgers on page 113 and shape the mixture into small balls instead of burgers.
> The balls are delicious to eat as they are, but can also be fried over a medium heat in a little vegetable oil until golden brown.

*PS ...*

*Of course, you can use many of the accompaniments, such as the Beetroot/beet Balls, Pesto and Kale, for other dinners or lunches. A useful tip is that you can freeze the beetroot balls after you have rolled them, before frying, and use them defrosted at a later time.*

# GROUNDING FOODS

Sometimes when we are stressed or feeling run-down, we may need food that's a little heartier to feel more grounded in our physical body. If you also have a tendency to become anxious and get caught up in overthinking, it is nice to have hot food that brings you back into your body. Served with fresh green salad, raw food or sprouts, it will still generate a feeling of freshness and balance. Drink a warm infusion with the food to facilitate digestion.

# BANANA AND CHICKPEA CURRY WITH RAISINS AND ROASTED CASHEWS

**SERVES 3–4**

1 onion, cut into wedges
2 tablespoons cold-pressed coconut oil
2 teaspoons ground cumin
2 teaspoons yellow curry powder
1 teaspoon ground coriander
1 red chilli, deseeded and sliced
4 ripe bananas, sliced
1 tablespoon vegetable stock/bouillon powder
300ml/10½fl oz/1¼ cups water
400g/14oz can chickpeas/garbanzo beans, rinsed
    and drained
sea salt flakes and freshly ground black pepper

TO SERVE
fresh coriander/cilantro
lime wedges
raisins
roasted cashews

> Fry the onion wedges in the coconut oil and
  sprinkle over the ground spices. Add the chilli
  and sliced bananas and fry around in the spiced
  oil. Sprinkle over the stock/bouillon powder
  and pour over the water. Let everything simmer,
  while stirring, for about 10 minutes.
> Add the chickpeas/garbanzo beans and let them
  warm through in the curry.
> Season to taste. If the sauce has become too
  thick, thin with a little more water.
> Serve with plenty of fresh coriander/cilantro,
  lime wedges, raisins and roasted cashews.
  Good served with quinoa and brown rice.

# LENTIL STEW WITH CINNAMON, LEMON AND THYME

**SERVES 3–4**

3½ tablespoons vegetable oil
1 large onion, cut into wedges
4 garlic cloves, peeled
300g/10½oz/1¾ cups green lentils (organic,
    if possible)
6 bay leaves
1 large cinnamon stick
1 large handful of fresh thyme
1 tablespoon vegetable stock/bouillon powder
(or a crumbled vegetable stock cube)
600ml/21fl oz/2½ cups water, plus more
    as needed
grated zest of 1 organic lemon
extra virgin olive oil, to drizzle
sea salt flakes and freshly ground black pepper

> Start by heating the vegetable oil in a heavy
  saucepan over a medium-high heat.
> Now add the onion, garlic, lentils, bay leaves,
  cinnamon stick and half the thyme.
> Let everything glaze with the oil and fry until the
  onion becomes a little softer. Stir frequently.
> Add the stock/bouillon powder (or cube) and
  then pour in the water.
> Let it simmer over a low heat for about 20
  minutes (check the amount of water half-way
  through and add a little extra if needed), or
  until the lentils are soft but still with some bite.
> Remove the cinnamon stick and bay leaves.
  Stir in the lemon zest and the rest of the thyme.
> Mash the soft garlic cloves and stir into the
  stew.
> Season generously and drizzle with good olive
  oil before serving.
> Serve lukewarm for the best flavour. Good with
  a green salad, tomatoes and a little crumbled
  vegan feta cheese.

# RAINBOW LASAGNE

**SERVES 4**

### TOMATO SAUCE
1 teaspoon extra virgin olive oil
2 garlic cloves, thinly sliced
400g/14oz can crushed tomatoes
6 large basil leaves, finely shredded
1 teaspoon agave syrup (optional)
1 large pinch each of sea salt flakes and freshly ground black pepper

> Heat the olive oil in a frying pan over a medium heat and let the garlic soften in the oil (without taking on any colour).
> Pour over the tomatoes and add the rest of the ingredients.
> Let the sauce simmer over a low heat for about 10 minutes.

### BEETROOT SAUCE
2 medium beetroots/beets, peeled and cut into small cubes
50g/1¾oz vegan feta
sea salt flakes and freshly ground black pepper

> Boil the beetroot/beet cubes in a saucepan of lightly salted water until soft, then drain.
> In a food processor, blitz the beetroot with the vegan feta until fully combined.
> Season to taste.

### SPINACH PESTO
1 large handful of fresh spinach leaves (about 35g/1¼oz)
8 large basil leaves
60g/2¼oz/½ cup pine nuts
3 tablespoons extra virgin olive oil
1 garlic clove, crushed
½ teaspoon sea salt flakes
a few grinds of black pepper

> Mix everything in a blender to a coarse pesto.

### TO ASSEMBLE
Tomato Sauce (see left)
gluten-free lasagne sheets or bean lasagne sheets
Beetroot Sauce (see left)
Spinach Pesto (see left)
oat cream or other plant-based cream
vegan Parmesan, grated

> Preheat the oven to 200°C/400°F/gas 6.
> Start by covering the bottom of a baking dish with a thin layer of the tomato sauce.
> Then add a layer of lasagne sheets.
> Spread the beetroot sauce over the top to cover.
> Then add another layer of lasagne sheets.
> Spread the spinach pesto over these so that it completely covers them.
> Spread with the remaining tomato sauce and top with a final layer of lasagne sheets.
> Pour a little oat cream along the edges and also sprinkle a little over the lasagne sheets.
> Top with a thin layer of vegan Parmesan.
> Bake for about 30 minutes, or until golden brown.
> Allow to cool slightly before serving with a large green salad, bean sprouts and grated carrots.

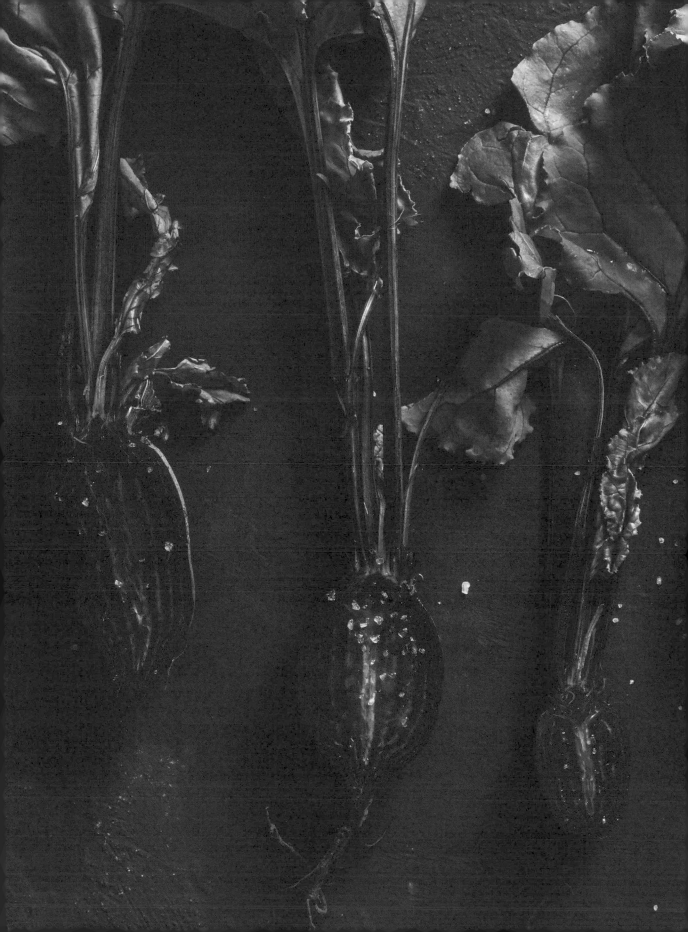

# GNOCCHI WITH ORANGE, SAFFRON AND CHILLI

**SERVES 2–4**

2½ tablespoons extra virgin olive oil
3 garlic cloves, thinly sliced
¼ teaspoon chilli flakes
1 pinch of saffron
1 teaspoon chopped fresh rosemary
zest of 1 organic orange, plus orange slices
    to serve
1 teaspoon sea salt flakes
a few grinds of black pepper
1 pack of gnocchi, preferably gluten-free
    (about 500g/1lb 2oz)
rocket/arugula, to serve

> Heat the olive oil in a frying pan over a medium-high heat.
> Let the garlic and chilli flakes soften in the oil without the garlic taking on any colour.
> Sprinkle with the saffron and rosemary. Then add the orange zest, salt and pepper.
> Stir and remove from the heat. Meanwhile, cook the gnocchi as directed on the packaging.
> Let the gnocchi drain quickly and then add it to the frying pan to coat in the saffron oil. Serve on a hearty bed of rocket/arugula leaves with a few orange slices on the side.
> Also good sprinkled with grated vegan Parmesan and extra black pepper.

# LAYERED LEBANESE AUBERGINE AND TOMATO CASSEROLE WITH MINT SAUCE

**SERVES 2–4**

**BAKED AUBERGINE/EGGPLANT**

2 medium aubergines/eggplants, cut lengthways into thin slices
a little extra virgin olive oil
1 pinch of sea salt flakes

> Preheat the oven to 220°C/425°F/gas 7.
> Place the aubergine slices on a wire/cooling rack and bake for about 10 minutes, or until lightly browned.
> Transfer to a plate, drizzle with a little olive oil and sprinkle with the sea salt flakes.

**SPICY TOMATO SAUCE**

1 tablespoon extra virgin olive oil
4 garlic cloves, thinly sliced
2 teaspoons ground cumin
1 teaspoon ground cinnamon
400g/14oz can crushed tomatoes
1 teaspoon harissa paste
1 teaspoon agave syrup
1–1½ teaspoons sea salt flakes

> Heat the olive oil in a frying pan over a medium-high heat.
> Let the garlic soften in the oil without the garlic taking on any colour.
> Sprinkle in the cumin and cinnamon and stir into the oil.
> Pour over the tomatoes, harissa and agave syrup and add sea salt flakes to taste.
> Let it simmer for 10 minutes over a low heat.

**MINT SAUCE**

1 handful of fresh mint
2 tablespoons extra virgin olive oil
2 tablespoons oat fraîche (or other vegan crème fraîche)
2 tablespoons water
¼ teaspoon sea salt flakes

> Blitz everything together in a blender or food processor until fully combined.

**TO ASSEMBLE**

Spicy Tomato Sauce (see left)
Baked Aubergine/eggplant (see left)
vegan Parmesan, grated
Mint Sauce (see left and above)

> Preheat the oven to 220°C/425°F/gas 7.
> Start with a thin layer of spicy tomato sauce at the bottom of a high-sided baking dish.
> Add a layer of baked aubergine/eggplant slices so they cover the tomato sauce.
> Spread another layer of spicy tomato sauce over the aubergine slices.
> Sprinkle a thin layer of grated vegan Parmesan over the tomato sauce. Then add another layer of baked aubergine slices.
> Finish with a final layer of tomato sauce and a sprinkling of vegan Parmesan.
> Bake for about 20–25 minutes. Cut into portions, then serve with a large green salad and drizzle with the mint sauce.
> Lovely to serve with honeydew melon and walnuts.

# BLACK RICE WITH PORTOBELLO MUSHROOMS, PAK CHOI, GARLIC, CORIANDER AND CHILLI

**SERVES 2**

2 medium portobello mushrooms, finely sliced
1½ teaspoons extra virgin olive oil
3 garlic cloves, thinly sliced
¼ teaspoon chilli flakes
1 head of pak choi/bok choy, well rinsed and cut into large pieces
1 tablespoon tamari soy sauce
200g/7oz/1½ cups cooked black rice, hot
1 handful of fresh coriander/cilantro, coarsely chopped
sea salt flakes and freshly ground black pepper
lime wedges, to serve

> Heat a dry frying pan over a medium heat.
> Place the mushroom slices in the pan so that they are separate. Let them get a little colour on both sides.
> Add the olive oil, garlic and chilli flakes and fry everything without the garlic taking on any colour. Add the pak choi/bok choy and let it soften slightly. Now pour in the tamari soy sauce. Season to taste.
> Finally, mix in the hot black rice and sprinkle generously with the coriander/cilantro. Serve hot and with wedges of lime on the side.

# QUINOA BOWL WITH MANDARIN, HAZELNUT, POMEGRANATE, ROSEMARY AND BRUSSELS SPROUTS

**SERVES 2–4**

**BRUSSELS SPROUTS**
500g/1lb 2oz Brussels sprouts, bases trimmed and outer leaves removed
2 teaspoons extra virgin olive oil
grated zest and juice of 1 mandarin
1 pinch of chopped fresh rosemary
sea salt flakes and freshly ground black pepper

> Preheat the oven to 220°C/425°F/gas 7. Halve the Brussels sprouts and place in a baking dish, with the cut sides facing up.
> Sprinkle the olive oil and mandarin zest and juice all over the sprouts. Sprinkle over the chopped rosemary.
> Season generously.
> Bake for about 20 minutes, or until coloured.

**QUINOA WITH MANDARIN AND CINNAMON**
200g/7oz/1 cup cooked and cooled quinoa
1 mandarin, peeled and sliced
½ red onion, thinly sliced
¼ teaspoon ground cinnamon
1 pinch of cayenne pepper

> Stir everything together in a bowl.

**GLAZED HAZELNUTS**
100g/3½oz/¾ cup hazelnuts
¼ teaspoon extra virgin olive oil
1 tablespoon agave syrup
1 pinch of ground cinnamon
1 pinch of sea salt flakes

> Roast the nuts in a dry frying pan. Pay attention so they do not burn.
> Drizzle over the olive oil and agave syrup, and turn the nuts so they are glazed.
> Sprinkle over the cinnamon and salt. Set aside.

**TO ASSEMBLE**
Quinoa with Mandarin and Cinnamon (see left)
Brussels Sprouts (see left)
green leaves (optional)
pomegranate seeds
Glazed Hazelnuts (see above)

> Stir the quinoa mixture into the Brussels sprouts to combine.
> Serve the quinoa and sprouts mixture on a bed of green leaves, if you like.
> Top with pomegranate seeds and the glazed hazelnuts.

# FILO BUNDLES WITH DIP

**EACH FILLING RECIPE MAKES 6
FILO/PHYLLO PARCELS**

**THREE FILLINGS:**

### POTATO, CURRY, CORIANDER
### AND PEANUT

5 white organic potatoes (about 300g/10½oz),
    washed, peel left on, and cut into cubes
1 tablespoon cold-pressed coconut oil
1 onion, coarsely chopped
1 garlic clove, crushed
1½ tablespoons yellow curry powder
2 tablespoons oat milk
sea salt flakes, to taste
1 handful of fresh coriander/cilantro,
    coarsely chopped
50g/1¾oz/½ cup coarsely chopped
    roasted salted peanuts

> Boil the potato cubes in a pan of lightly
  salted water until soft. Drain well.
> Heat the coconut oil in a frying pan over
  a medium heat and fry the onion until softened.
> Add the potato, garlic and spices and
  fry for several minutes.
> Add oat milk and stir.
> Toss in the peanuts and coriander. Put aside.

### VEGAN FETA CHEESE, WALNUT
### AND MINT

100g/3½oz/1 cup raw walnuts
80g/2¾oz vegan feta cheese
½ garlic clove, crushed
1 teaspoon dried mint
1 small pinch each of sea salt flakes
    and freshly ground black pepper

> Mix everything until fully combined.

### SUN-DRIED TOMATO, OLIVE
### AND SWEET POTATO

1 sweet potato (about 200g/7oz), peeled
    and cut into cubes
2 teaspoons extra virgin olive oil
1 garlic clove, crushed
½ teaspoon dried thyme
15 kalamata olives, pitted and sliced
10 sun-dried tomatoes in oil, cut into strips
sea salt flakes and freshly ground black pepper

> Boil the sweet potato cubes in a pan of lightly
  salted water until soft. Drain well.
> Heat the olive oil in a frying pan over a
  medium-high heat and let the garlic soften in
  the oil without it taking on any colour.
> Add the sweet potatoes and mash with a fork
  in the garlic oil.
> Season with the thyme, and salt and pepper.
> Finally, stir in the olives and tomatoes.

### GARLIC DIP

200g/7oz/scant 1 cup oat sour cream
1 small garlic clove, crushed
1 tablespoon extra virgin olive oil
sea salt flakes and freshly ground black pepper

> Mix everything together thoroughly.

### TO ASSEMBLE

gluten-free filo/phyllo pastry sheets
cold-pressed coconut oil
your choice of filling (see left)
Garlic Dip (see above)

> Preheat the oven to 200°C/400°F/gas 6.
> Take 2 sheets of filo/phyllo pastry and put them
  together. Brush them generously with coconut
  oil, especially at the edges.
> Cut into 6 large squares. Place a spoonful of the
  filling in the centre of each square and gather
  up the corners to meet in the middle. Use some
  coconut oil to seal into a small package.
> Place your finished packages on a baking sheet
  lined with baking parchment.
> Bake for about 10 minutes, or until golden
  brown and crispy. Allow to cool slightly before
  serving with the garlic dip.
> Good with a green salad. Also good to serve
  as tapas along with other small dishes.

# NATURAL DESSERTS FROM MOTHER EARTH

To create balance is also to allow oneself to enjoy the sweetness of life that warms the soul. When we eat with a positive energy, it in turn creates positive energy in our body. Therefore, enjoy fully when you eat. We humans have a natural attraction to the sweet from childhood, and nature's pantry has an abundance of natural goodies to offer. These goodies still give you a light feeling and good energy. They are suitable for both everyday and more festive occasions. They are also fun to make for all ages.

# RAW HEARTS

**EACH RECIPE MAKES ABOUT 10 HEARTS**

## VANILLA, TAHINI AND RASPBERRY

100g/3½oz/generous ¾ cup raw cashews
2 tablespoons cold-pressed coconut oil, in solid form
4 Medjool dates, pitted
3 tablespoons grated coconut
1 teaspoon unsweetened vanilla powder
3 tablespoons tahini
2 tablespoons freeze-dried raspberry powder
1 tablespoon sesame seeds
¼ teaspoon sea salt flakes
1 teaspoon agave syrup

> Blitz the cashews into a flour in a food processor.
> Add the rest of the ingredients and mix well to make a firm dough.
> Leave it in the refrigerator for 5–10 minutes.
> Roll out on baking parchment and use a mini cutter to press out 10 hearts.

## CACAO AND SEA SALT FLAKES

200g/7oz/2 cups gluten-free porridge/ rolled oats (or 200g/7oz/2 cups walnuts)
100g/3½oz/1½ cups grated coconut
3 tablespoons cold-pressed coconut oil, in solid form
8 Medjool dates, pitted
2 tablespoons raw cacao powder, plus extra for dusting
1 teaspoon unsweetened vanilla powder
½ teaspoon sea salt flakes
1 teaspoon agave syrup

> Blitz the oats (or nuts) into a flour in a food processor.
> Add the rest of the ingredients and mix well to make a firm dough.
> Leave it in the refrigerator for 5–10 minutes.
> Roll out on baking parchment and use a mini cutter to press out 10 hearts.
> Dust with a little raw cacao powder to finish.

## LEMON AND CARDAMOM

100g/3½oz/generous ¾ cup raw cashews
2 tablespoons melted cacao butter
4 Medjool dates, pitted
1 teaspoon unsweetened vanilla powder
1 tablespoon ground cardamom
2 tablespoons sesame seeds
1 tablespoon grated coconut
grated zest of 1 organic lemon
¼ teaspoon sea salt flakes
1–2 teaspoons agave syrup, to taste

> Blitz the cashews into a flour in a food processor
> Add the rest of the ingredients and mix well to make a firm dough.
> Leave it in the refrigerator for 5–10 minutes.
> Roll out on baking parchment and use a mini cutter to press out 10 hearts.

*PS ...*

*These raw hearts last about a week stored in an airtight container in the refrigerator. They are also perfect to freeze and defrost when needed. In my house, we are crazy about the cacao and sea salt flakes variation and make these together in minimal time when the craving sets in! It's a fun activity for everyone.*

**Vanilla powder**

**Coconut flakes**

**Medjool dates**

**Sea salt**

**Cashews**

**Freeze-dried raspberry powder**

**Tahini**

**Coconut oil**

# PSYCHEDELIC CHIA

**SERVES 1**

**IN EACH GLASS:**
1 layer of Pink Chia (see below)
1 layer of Yellow Chia (see below)
1 layer of Purple Chia (see right)
Raw Frosting (see right)
1 slice of nectarine, peach or persimmon
2 pineapple leaves
3 fresh blueberries

> Put a layer of pink chia in the bottom of a transparent glass and flatten with a spoon.
> Then put a layer of yellow chia on top, flatten it and add a layer of purple chia.
> Pipe a generous rosette of raw frosting on top of the purple layer.
> Add the nectarine slice and 2 pineapple leaves.
> Decorate with the blueberries.

**PINK CHIA**
2 tablespoons chia seeds
100ml/3½fl oz/scant ½ cup sweet almond milk
    or coconut milk
½ teaspoon agave syrup
1 teaspoon freeze-dried raspberry powder
¼ teaspoon ground cardamom
¼ teaspoon unsweetened vanilla powder

> Whisk all the ingredients in a bowl and let the mixture swell for 4 hours.

**YELLOW CHIA**
2 tablespoons chia seeds
100ml/3½fl oz/scant ½ cup sweet almond milk
    or coconut milk
½ teaspoon agave syrup
1 teaspoon freeze-dried passion fruit powder
¼ teaspoon unsweetened vanilla powder

> Whisk all the ingredients in a bowl and let the mixture swell for 4 hours.

**PURPLE CHIA**
2 tablespoons chia seeds
100ml/3½fl oz/scant ½ cup sweet almond milk
    or coconut milk
½ teaspoon agave syrup
1 teaspoon freeze-dried blueberry powder
¼ teaspoon ground cardamom
¼ teaspoon unsweetened vanilla powder

> Whisk all the ingredients in a bowl and let the mixture swell for 4 hours.

**RAW FROSTING**
300g/10½oz/2½ cups raw cashews, soaked
    for at least 4 hours, then drained
freshly squeezed juice of 2 lemons
3½ tablespoons cold-pressed coconut oil
3½ tablespoons water
3½ tablespoons agave syrup
¼ teaspoon blue spirulina powder

> Blitz everything in a food processor to make a smooth cream.
> Pour into a piping/pastry bag fitted with an open star tip and leave in the refrigerator to solidify slightly before piping.

# NICECREAM CONE

**SERVES 4–6**

### BLUEBERRY AND CINNAMON

3 ripe frozen bananas, cut into large pieces
   (slightly defrosted)
200g/7oz/1½ cups frozen blueberries
1 teaspoon ground cinnamon
1 teaspoon coconut sugar or agave syrup

> Blitz everything in a food processor to make a
  smooth nicecream.
> Scoop into balls on gluten-free cones.

### STRAWBERRY AND CARDAMOM

3 ripe frozen bananas, cut into large pieces
   (slightly defrosted)
300g/10½oz/2 cups frozen strawberries
½ teaspoon ground cardamom
1 teaspoon coconut sugar or agave syrup

> Blitz everything in a food processor to make
  a smooth nicecream.
> Scoop into balls on gluten-free cones.

### MANGO AND COCONUT

1 ripe frozen banana, cut into large pieces
   (slightly defrosted)
400g/14oz frozen mango
50g/1¾oz/¾ cup grated coconut
4 tablespoons coconut cream
1 teaspoon coconut sugar or agave syrup

> Blitz everything in a food processor to make
  a smooth nicecream.
> Scoop into balls on gluten-free cones.

*PS ...*

*Use really ripe bananas for the nicecream. Cut them into pieces and place in the freezer. Can be used for nicecream, Love Bowls (see page 86) or smoothies. Sprinkle your nicecream with grated coconut and cacao nibs. Or make a nicecream bowl and top with Raw Hearts (see page 143), a dollop of coconut cream, Raw Caramel Dip (see page 155) and fresh berries. It will put a smile on everyone's face!*

# RHUBARB, STRAWBERRY AND COCONUT DREAM

**SERVES 4**

**IN EACH GLASS:**
a few Strawberry Slices (see below)
a layer of Rhubarb and Strawberry Purée
   (see below)
a layer of coconut yogurt or coconut cream
Glazed Pecans (see right)

**STRAWBERRY SLICES**
4 strawberries

> Slice each strawberry thinly lengthways from the highest point, to get the heart shape.

**RHUBARB AND STRAWBERRY PURÉE**
1 large rhubarb stalk, washed and cut into small
   pieces
3 fresh strawberries, chopped, plus extra
(optional) to decorate
3½ tablespoons water
3½ tablespoons agave syrup
2 tablespoons coconut sugar
½ teaspoon ground cinnamon

> Let all the ingredients simmer together in a small saucepan over a low heat for about 10 minutes.
> Everything should simmer down into a thick mixture.
> Allow to cool until just lukewarm.

**GLAZED PECANS**
100g/3½oz/1 cup pecans
2 teaspoons agave syrup
½ teaspoon ground cinnamon
¼ teaspoon sea salt flakes

> Heat a non-stick frying pan over a medium heat.
> Roast the pecans in the pan without allowing them to take on any colour.
> Drizzle over the agave syrup and sprinkle over the cinnamon and salt.
> Stir and turn the nuts over until the agave syrup melts and the nuts are coated.
> Spread out and allow to cool on baking parchment.

**TO ASSEMBLE**
> Place a layer of strawberry slices over the base and around the sides of each glass.
> Add a good layer of rhubarb and strawberry purée so that it covers the sliced strawberries.
> Place a layer of coconut yogurt or coconut cream over the purée.
> Top with the glazed pecans, and a few pieces of chopped strawberry, if you like.

# RAW PASTRY CUP WITH BLUEBERRY FROSTING

**MAKES 10–15 PASTRIES**

1 batch of Cacao and Sea Salt Flakes Raw Heart
  Dough (see page 143)
1 batch of Frosting with Blueberries (see right)
fresh blueberries, to decorate
small flowers, to decorate

> Divide the dough into 10–15 small balls and
  press your thumb into the middle of each so
  you can shape them into small, flat cups. Place
  them in serving plates or bowls.
> Cover each dough cup with piped frosting
  and then decorate with fresh blueberries and
  flowers (see picture).

**FROSTING WITH BLUEBERRIES**
300g/10½oz/2½ cups raw cashews
100ml/3½fl oz/scant ½ cup freshly squeezed
  lemon juice
3 tablespoons frozen blueberries, defrosted
100ml/3½fl oz/scant ½ cup agave syrup
5 tablespoons melted cold-pressed coconut oil
1 teaspoon grated organic lemon zest
1 teaspoon unsweetened vanilla powder

> Blitz the nuts in a food processor to a flour.
> Add the rest of the ingredients. First mix
  everything using the "pulse" button and then
  mix more thoroughly and for a long time until it
  becomes really fluffy and absolutely no traces
  of the nuts are visible (a teaspoon of water may
  be needed to get it all started).
> Pour the frosting into a piping/pastry bag
  fitted with an open star tip and store in the
  refrigerator until ready to use.

# PINEAPPLE SKEWERS WITH RAW CARAMEL DIP

**MAKES 1 SKEWER**

8 bite-size pieces of fresh pineapple (also good to vary with berries and other tropical fruits)
coconut flakes

RAW CARAMEL DIP
3 Medjool dates, pitted
3 tablespoons maple syrup or agave syrup
1 teaspoon cold-pressed coconut oil
2 teaspoons water
½ teaspoon sea salt flakes

> Thread the pineapple pieces onto a skewer and sprinkle with some coconut flakes.
> Put all the ingredients for the dip in a food processor or blender and blitz to a smooth consistency, then pour into a bowl.
> Serve the skewer with the raw caramel dip.

*PS ...*

*Did you know that a sun-ripened pineapple is filled with highly vibrating and uplifting energy? The fruit stores the solar energy when it ripens on the tree, and when we eat it, we get this wonderful life force into our energy system.*

# LIQUID BALANCE

We all know that it is important to balance our body with plenty of water. We help the body cleanse itself from toxins, regulate the temperature, and maintain elasticity in the skin. Water is pure life force; it causes our cells to communicate with each other, because water conducts energy, and keeps our energy replenished.

Buy a jug or a pitcher with a carbon filter to improve the quality of your drinking water.

In many cultures, different ceremonies are performed to bless the water, by singing and giving flowers and gratitude. It is claimed that the molecules of the water respond to the positive energy and further activate the life force in the water. For those of us in more urban cultures, we can stop for a second and feel grateful that we have fresh running water before we drink it. This is a great way to be a little more aware of how amazing Mother Earth is, to provide us with its resources daily.

To create calm and cleanse yourself from negativity you swhould listen to water sounds, take soothing baths and sit by streams. It helps you bring more flow into life and balances activity and tranquillity.

## COCONUT WATER

Coconut water is nature's own energy drink and electrolyte fluid, which awakens the body and deeply moisturizes it. It transfers energy between our cells and gives them a form of "electrical charge" that promotes communication between all cells in your body.

Coconut water is full of minerals and salts that the body needs which are usually lost through sweat. It helps the body to speed up the whole cell renewal process and keeps us free from waste and toxins. Drink coconut water in its pure form or try to make playful cocktails and smoothies. I cannot get enough of this amazing drink!

# COCO COCKTAILS WITH COCONUT WATER, FRUITS, BERRIES AND HERBS

**ALL RECIPES SERVE 1**

### SUMMER VIBE
350g/12oz watermelon, peeled
1 hearty pinch of fresh mint
100g/3½oz/¾ cup frozen strawberries
200ml/7fl oz/scant 1 cup coconut water
2 large ice cubes

> Blitz everything in a blender.

### PIÑA COCO
350g/12oz ripe pineapple, peeled and woody
    core removed
freshly squeezed juice of ½ lime
a hearty pinch of fresh mint
200ml/7fl oz/scant 1 cup coconut water
2 large ice cubes

>Blitz everything in a blender.

### COCO GREEN
4 sweet pears, with peel
1 kiwi, peeled
¼ lime, with peel
1 hearty pinch of fresh mint
¼ teaspoon wheatgrass powder
100ml/3½fl oz/scant ½ cup coconut water
2 large ice cubes

> Squeeze the pears, kiwi and lime in a
  centrifugal juicer.
> Pour the fruit juice into your blender along with
  the rest of the ingredients, and mix.

### COCONUT WATER WITH LEMON, LAVENDER AND MINT
1 slice of lemon with peel
1 sprig of fresh mint
2 sprigs of fresh lavender with flowers
300ml/10½fl oz/1¼ cups cold coconut water

> Let everything infuse for 5–7 minutes.

### COCONUT WATER WITH ROSEBUDS, BLUEBERRIES AND CARDAMOM
1 teaspoon dried rosebuds (available from health-
    food stores or specialist tea suppliers)
1 tablespoon fresh blueberries
7 whole cardamom pods
300ml/10½fl oz/1¼ cups cold coconut water

> Let everything infuse for 5–7 minutes.

# HERBAL AND SPICE INFUSIONS

Humans have always used herbs and spices for their various effects. These infusions both calm and give renewed energy to your chakras while being fully adaptable to your needs. Prepare a jug/pitcher and sip on the infusions during the day, or take soothing herbs in the evening for better sleep. Let herbs be a part of your everyday life.

## EACH RECIPE MAKES 1 LARGE CUP

### THE ROOT CHAKRA
3cm/1¼in piece of fresh ginger, sliced
2 sprigs of fresh mint
400ml/14fl oz/1²/₃ cups hot boiled water

> Let it all infuse for 5 minutes. Benefits: activates the energy of the root chakra. The mint calms and the ginger stimulates.

### THE SACRAL CHAKRA
10 whole cardamom pods
1 teaspoon whole fennel seeds
½ teaspoon unsweetened vanilla powder
400ml/14fl oz/1²/₃ cups hot boiled water

> Let it infuse for 5 minutes. Benefits: calms the digestive system. Warming and soothing.

### THE SOLAR PLEXUS CHAKRA
1 thick slice of organic orange with peel
1 cinnamon stick
8 whole cloves
400ml/14fl oz/1²/₃ cups hot boiled water

> Let it infuse for 5 minutes. Benefits: helps combustion to get started. Good if you have stomach ailments.

### THE HEART CHAKRA
1 tablespoon dried rosebuds (available from health-food stores or specialist tea suppliers)
400ml/14fl oz/1¾ cups hot boiled water

> Let it all infuse for 5 minutes. Benefits: opens the heart. Arouses feelings of love, provides comfort in times of grief, raises awareness.

### THE THROAT CHAKRA
2 sprigs of fresh mint
2 sprigs of dried sage
1 slice of organic lemon with peel
400ml/14fl oz/1²/₃ cups hot boiled water

> Let it all infuse for 5 minutes. Benefits: cleanses the throat, gives a clearer voice. Good during cold season, preferably with 1 tablespoon agave syrup.

### THE THIRD EYE CHAKRA
2 sprigs of fresh lavender with flowers
1 teaspoon dried lavender
2 sprigs of fresh rosemary
400ml/14fl oz/1²/₃ cups hot boiled water

> Let it all infuse for 5 minutes. Benefits: provides clarity and mental peace. Removes negativity and raises the mind.

### THE CROWN CHAKRA
1 slice of organic lemon with peel
1 teaspoon dried rosebuds (available from health-food stores or specialist tea suppliers)
400ml/14fl oz/1²/₃ cups hot boiled water

> Let it all infuse for 5 minutes. Benefits: activates high vibration and an open mind.

Crown Chakra

Third Eye
Chakra

Throat Chakra

Heart Chakra

Solar Plexus
Chakra

Sacral Chakra

Root Chakra

# GOOD NIGHT

Are you among those who fall asleep late with their heads full of to-do lists and worrying about how to keep up with everything? Get a cozy evening routine that gives you a deeper rest at night and thus a more efficient day. Sleep and rest are really the body's way of recovering, regenerating itself at the cellular level and getting rid of what no longer benefits it. We can help the body with this process. Make it a loving ritual with yourself.

- Let your stomach rest from heavy food after 8pm.
- If you have been feeling heavy and tired throughout the day, replace your dinner with a chakra smoothie.
- Sip the Third Eye Infusion Chakra (see page 160).
- Ashwagandha is a balancing superfood for a good night's sleep. Try a Turmeric Latte (see page 81) and then add ½–1 teaspoon of a Ashwagandha powder.
- An aroma diffuser with lavender scent makes the air in the bedroom more pleasant.
- Light some candles, turn on relaxing music and consider having amethyst crystals in your bedroom. They help absorb heavy energy and provide peace in the room.
- If you have a lot on your mind, place a notebook by your bed so you can write everything down exactly as it is right now, without filtering or beautifying it. If life is difficult and stressful, let it flow out on the paper. To not get caught up in what has already been, you can then tear out your pages and set them on fire (if you have a fireplace and can do so safely). It does not have to be complicated; it is the intention that is important. The key thing is that everything must come out of you and that you can then let go of what has been.
- Now you can sit comfortably in your bed and do your gratitude exercise (see page 166).

*PS ...* Ashwagandha is a fantastically powerful superfood from India that has been used in Ayurveda for a long time. It reduces stress, anxiety and depression. It has anti-inflammatory effects and builds up the immune system. Because it has a calming and rebuilding effect on your energy system, it is perfect to take in the evening. However, this is not suitable for pregnant women, who can instead drink the soothing third eye lavender infusion (see page 160).

# GRATITUDE—MINDFULNESS EXERCISE TO END THE DAY

This simple exercise is great for changing the energy in your body. It's perfect to end the day with so you have a good feeling to bring with you into your dreams. It does not have to take a long time. Sometimes the simplest tools are the most powerful once we make them a part of our everyday lives.

**STEP 1**

Sit comfortably, in a position that allows a straight spine and relaxed shoulders.

Relax your entire face and take a few deep breaths in through your nose and out through your mouth. For each exhalation, you exhale everything that has been during the day to land fully in the present. It is optional to close your eyes.

**STEP 2**

Now focus all your presence on the point between your eyebrows, the third eye, and take a few deep breaths. See for your inner self what you already have in your life that gives you joy (partner, friend, child, place, pet, hobby, etc.). See it in front of you and feel the joy it gives. Feel grateful for the joy you have in your life.

**STEP 3**

Now focus all your presence on your throat chakra, the point in the middle of the throat. Take a few deep breaths. Now see for your inner self something that is unique in your own expression. A gift that you have and love to express yourself with, or something that you have a penchant for (good at listening, writing, cooking, dancing, being a parent, being loving, a professional role, etc.). Honour that part of yourself and feel grateful that you have received this gift and means of expression.

**STEP 4**

Now focus all your presence on your heart chakra, the point between your breasts, and take deep breaths here. See for your inner self the love you already have in your life (it can be for yourself, a partner, your children, a place, a pet, a friend, etc.). Feel how that love is in your life and the feeling it gives you. Feel grateful that you have this love in your life. Stay with this feeling of warmth, love and gratitude that can fill the whole body. If you have closed your eyes, open them slowly when you feel ready.

 *Once you feel safe in this exercise, you can be creative and do it in a way that feels most natural to you. The most important thing is that you awaken the gratitude inside yourself and really feel. The more you find to be grateful for in the life you already have in the present, the more flows into your life to be grateful for. This is a universal principle.*

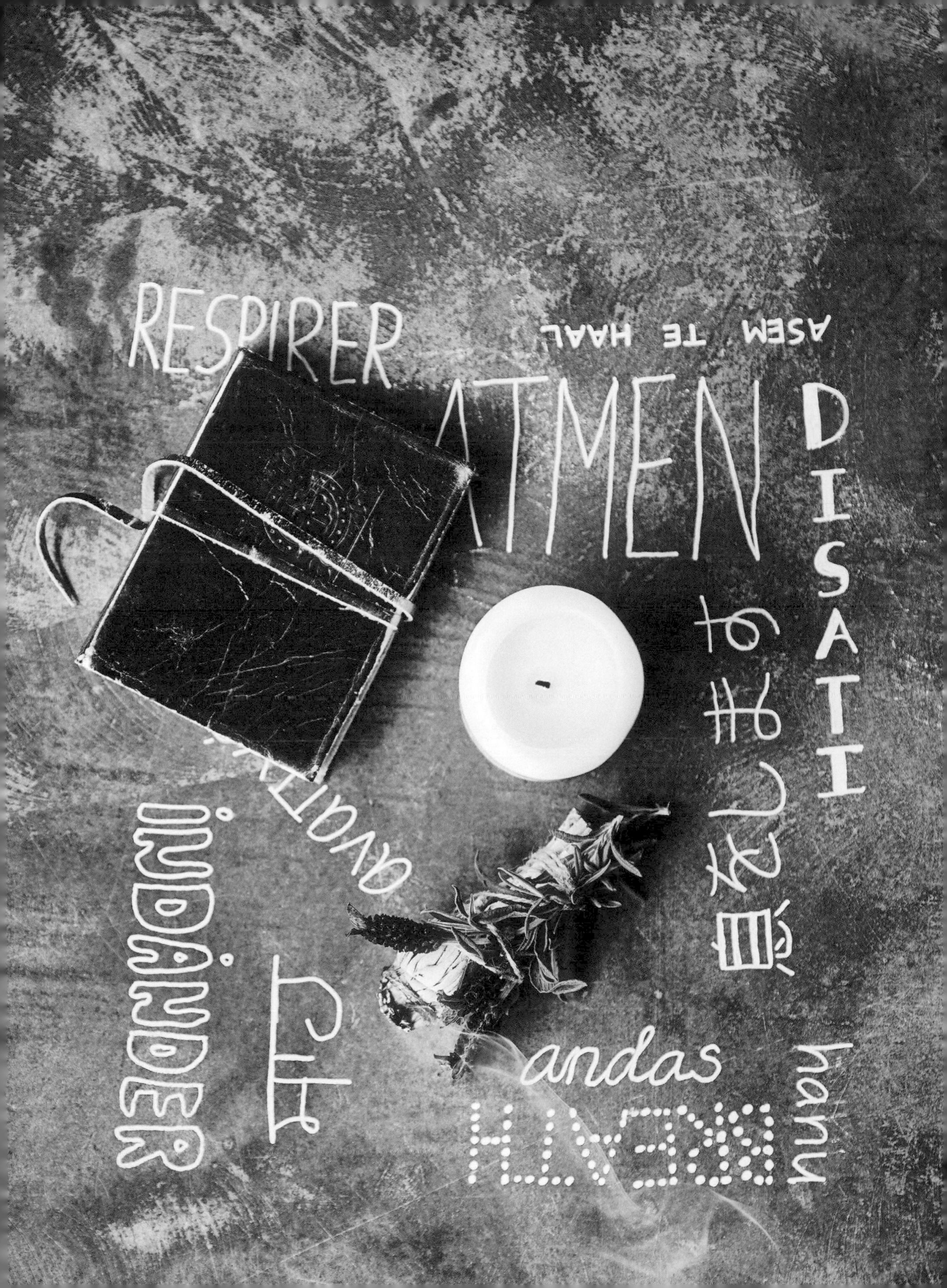
RESPIRER
ATMEN
andas

# 5-DAY PROGRAMME — RESTART AND CHARGE YOURSELF WITH NEW ENERGY

If you have lived with stress, heavy food, fatigue and lack of energy for a long time, it's useful to reboot your energy. Sometimes it's difficult to track what puts your energy out of balance, and many times it can involve several combined components. On these occasions, it can feel good to start with a "blank page" and give the body extra love. Our body has an amazing ability to recover and wants to function as well as possible. Our cleansing organs work around the clock to remove toxins from our body.

Here I offer a cleansing programme to regain energy and support the cleansing process in the body – an opportunity to find your own balance again, clear out heavy energy and replenish with new, wonderful power!

# DURING THESE DAYS:

- Make sure you take it easy and do not permit stress or be too physical. Listen to the body. If it wants to rest, then slow things down. In case of nausea during the first couple of days, you can drink boiling water with fresh ginger. The infusion for the root chakra is well suited to this (see page 160).
- Take a break from caffeinated coffee and drink decaffeinated instead, or a Rainbow Latte (see page 78).
- If you feel fit and strong, you can increase your body's energy through brisk walking or swimming.
- Remember to drink water between meals – approximately 250ml/9fl oz/1 cup of hot boiled water once an hour until dinner. Add infusions for extra advantages, from the Herbal and Spice Infusions section (see page 160).
- Drink water sparingly during meals. After dinner, a large cup of tea or infusion of soothing herbs before bedtime is enough.
- To feel motivated with your reboot, you can prepare as best as possible for this. Make sure you have all the ingredients. If you have a juicer, you can prepare your juices the night before. Always plan your meals at least a day in advance so it feels easier. If you do not have the energy to make different smoothies on the same day, then make a larger batch of the same smoothie for that day.

Always have the mindset of "What is possible?" instead of focusing on what you're not able to do.
- It is easy to start with too high demands of yourself and become too focused on results. Relax and leave everything as it is. You cannot control the body. It does what it needs to do to heal itself. See it as a gift to yourself and your body.

YOUR PROGRAMME:
DAY 1
> Start the day with a morning infusion, morning breath and intention for the day.
> You can take a quick morning walk before breakfast.

**Breakfast:** Heart chakra smoothie
**Snack:** Optional green juice
**Lunch:** Throat chakra smoothie
**Snack:** Optional green juice
**Dinner:** Solar plexus smoothie
**Evening:** Third eye infusion, ending with an exercise in gratitude

DAY 2
> Start the day with a morning infusion, morning breath and intention for the day.
> You can take a quick morning walk before breakfast.

**Breakfast:** Root chakra smoothie
**Snack:** Optional red or orange juice
**Lunch:** Third eye smoothie
**Snack:** Optional plant-based milk
**Dinner:** Solar plexus smoothie
**Evening:** Turmeric latte, ending with an exercise in gratitude

**DAY 3**
> Start the day with a morning infusion, morning breath and intention for the day.
> You can take a quick morning walk before breakfast.

**Breakfast:** "Purple dream" love bowl with 2 optional toppings
**Snack:** Optional red, green or orange juice
**Lunch:** Courgette swirl with citrus and pumpkin seed pesto
**Snack:** Cucumber and carrot sticks with hummus of your choice
**Dinner:** Asian ramen
**Evening:** Optional infusion, ending with an exercise in gratitude

**DAY 4**
> Start the day with a morning infusion, morning breath and intention for the day.
> You can take a quick morning walk before breakfast.
> Also add a workout or a brisk walk in the afternoon.

**Breakfast:** Optional green juice and a small bowl of coconut yogurt with salty cacao granola and berries.

**Snack:** Optional green juice
**Lunch:** Raw walnut mince in salad leaves topped with guacamole
**Snack:** Wheatgrass latte
**Dinner:** Cabbage leaf wraps with mango and tahini purée
**Evening:** Optional infusion, ending with an exercise in gratitude

**DAY 5**
> Start the day with a morning infusion, morning breath and intention for the day.
> You can take a quick morning walk before breakfast.
> Also add a workout or a brisk walk in the afternoon.

**Breakfast:** Third eye smoothie or "Sunshine" love bowl with berry topping
**Snack:** Optional red, green or orange juice
**Lunch:** Crown chakra smoothie
**Snack:** "High frequency" nut milk
**Dinner:** Fresh Vietnamese rolls with dip
**Evening:** Optional infusion, ending with an exercise in gratitude

*PS ...*

*This reboot is meant to inspire you, to help you discover how you can structure your days using the recipes in the book. You will get an amazing energy back! If it feels good, you can, of course, continue longer than five days. If it feels too challenging to only eat liquid food for the first two days, then choose one of the book's lunch or dinner recipes. Take care of yourself during this phase. See this as a reboot to give yourself a little extra love.*

# INSPIRATION FOR A CHAKRA KITCHEN PANTRY

Start slowly but surely replacing certain ingredients in your kitchen for a more energy-giving lifestyle. You do not have to buy everything at once or always have everything at home, but take one step at a time and review your basic foods. See it as an investment in yourself and your health!

It feels much easier to "throw together" a dish when you have a good basic range of energy-giving ingredients. Here you get an inspiration for what it can look like in the refrigerator, freezer and pantry.

## IN THE REFRIGERATOR:
- apple
- aubergine/eggplant
- avocado
- banana
- beetroot/beet
- blueberries
- broccoli
- brussels sprouts
- cabbage
- carrot
- celery
- coconut water
- courgette/zucchini
- fig
- fresh chilli
- fresh ginger
- fresh tumeric
- garlic
- kale
- kiwi
- lemon
- lime
- mango
- Medjool dates
- oat fraîche
- onion
- orange
- pineapple
- plant-based milk
- raspberries
- red cabbage
- spinach
- strawberries
- sugar snap peas
- sweet potato
- tomato

## IN THE FREEZER:
- blueberries
- frozen peeled bananas (cut into large pieces)
- peas
- mango
- papaya
- raspberries
- strawberries
- sweetcorn/corn kernels

## IN THE PANTRY:
- bicarbonate of soda/baking soda
- black beans
- cacoa nibs
- chickpeas/garbanzo beans
- coconut cream, coconut milk
- corn or rice cakes
- chopped tomatoes
- different seeds (chia, hemp, pumpkin, sunflower, sesame)
- gluten-free pasta
- gluten-free porridge/rolled oats
- granola
- peanut butter
- polenta/cornmeal
- quinoa
- raw apple cider vinegar
- raw nuts (Brazil nuts, cashews, macadamias, pecans, walnuts)
- red rice
- rice noodles
- rice paper
- rice vinegar
- tamari soy sauce
- vegetable stock/bouillon powder or cube

## DRIED HERBS AND SPICES:
- bay leaves
- black peppercorns
- cardamom
- cayene pepper
- chilli flakes
- chilli powder
- cinnamon
- cloves
- coriander
- cumin
- fennel seeds
- ginger
- liquorice powder
- mint
- oregano
- sage
- sea salt flakes, sea salt, rock salt

smoked paprika
thyme
turmeric
vanilla powder
yellow curry powder

### FRESH HERBS (GROW ON THE BALCONY/WINDOW IN SUMMER):

basil
coriander/cilantro
lavender
lemon balm
mint
rosemary
thyme

### FATS:

cacao butter
cold-pressed coconut oil
extra virgin olive oil
sesame oil
vegetable oil

### SWEETENERS:

agave syrup
coconut sugar

### SUPERFOODS:

acai powder
baobab powder
blueberry powder
blue spirulina powder
camu camu
maca
passion fruit powder
raspberry powder
raw cacao
spirulina powder
wheatgrass, barley grass

### SUPERFOODS (IF NEEDED):

ashwagandha
chaga
chlorella
cordyceps
ginseng
guarana
reishi mushrooms
schisandra

### EXCELLENT AIDS IN THE KITCHEN:

blender – for smoothies and coco cocktails
cold-press or centrifugal juicer – for juices
food processor – for mixing and sauces
mini cookie cutters – for shaped doughs
nut-milk bag – for making nut milk
piping/pastry bag – for raw frosting
vegetable spiralizer – to create noodles/pasta from vegetables, for example, courgette/zucchini
zester – for easy grating of citrus fruit peels for smoothies and desserts

# INDEX

Note: page numbers in bold refer to images.